Sparks
in the
Ether

A True Story about a Pioneer Radioman

Valarie J. Anderson

Sparks in the Ether*: A True Story about a Pioneer Radioman*
Creative non-fiction
History, Biography

Library of Congress Control Number 2023917198

Cover design: Germancreative at Fiverr.com

Voleander Press,
Sisters, Oregon
voleanderpress@gmail.com

Also by the author

Non-fiction
Money Eater:
Bernard Otto Kuehn

Pearl Harbor's Final Warning:
A Man, a Message and Paradise Lost

Blog
The Footfalls of History
www.valarieanderson.com

For
My clan

Table of Contents

George Street 1931

Preface

Sparks in the Ether is about George Street, my maternal grandfather. He was a pioneer wireless radio operator—a "Sparks"—who helped expand radio's worldwide wireless network when unfamiliar skies were referred to as the ether.

This book is a work of creative nonfiction and the prequel to my award-winning book, *Pearl Harbor's Final Warning*. All the events presented are accurate. George really did cut out his infected tattoo, encounter the Lindberghs while in China, and FDR at Warm Springs. The conversations, reactions, inner points of view, descriptions, and some settings are inferred but rooted in reality as allowed by this genre. Actual and overheard conversations are footnoted. My grandmother, Kay Street, really did say, "Would you—for a big red apple?" to my brand new husband—in jest, of course, but that was my Nana.

***

George Street braved the seas of change as a steam schooner radioman and later as a Radio Corporation of America (RCA) representative in the Pacific Northwest, Asia, and Hawaii. Fortunately, he saved his records, and my mother and uncle held onto them. I found part of his archive in a red suitcase under my mother's guest room bed.

His letters, documents, and pictures exposed the tough times of the early 20th Century when moral compasses swung radically between the Victorian past and the freedoms introduced by the Industrial Revolution—when men were men and women were *supposed* to be arm candy.

I only met George Street a handful of times. He was not approachable, did not delight in children, and had more to say about himself than others. First and foremost, he was a radioman, technologically and diplomatically. And he was proud of it. He was loyal to his firm and pleased by the fact that he helped connect the East with the West. Exacting, demanding, prideful, and controlling are the words that define him. But those traits also helped him survive.

My step-grandmother, Nina, is part of this story, too. She had even stricter standards—woe to the child who fuzzed her carpets with their trampling feet.

The grandparent I remember best is my maternal grandmother, Kay Street—my Nana. She was part of our household for more than fifty years. At one point, I shared a room with her. Nana was as complex as a fine piece of lace—charming, elegant, and vain, but a Flapper from the Roaring Twenties at heart. She loved being arm candy and the center of attention. Her vanity was legendary. As she aged, she put tape over her mirror, leaving only a space large enough to apply lipstick. She didn't want to see her wrinkles. And she was a flirt to the end. Nana embarrassed my mother, Barbara, and

Kay Street in her early 60s.
(Courtesy of Kathy Klattenhoff)

my father, Art, as much as she did George. An oft-heard refrain from my father was, "Barb, do something about your mother," like the time she told racy jokes at her 100th birthday party as we toasted her longevity with margaritas, her favorite drink.

I obtained much of my grandparent's story from their son, George Jr., who refused to see his mother, Kay, for thirty years. He finally let the skeletons out of the closet when he was in his late nineties. Newspaper articles, interviews, and George's archive filled in the blanks.

It took me years to unearth my grandparents' story and piece it together with some of wireless radio's history in the Pacific. Writing the unseen story of my grandparents and parents was difficult. Few imagine risqué behavior, passionate love, and betrayal when in the bosom of family love.

But the truth always makes the best tales. I learned a lot. And I hope you do, too.

Street Family

Johnson Ford Street 1855-1920
m. 1882 Wilhelmina (Schwerdt) Street 1857-1949

Johnson and Wilhelmina's children:

William Schwerdt Street 1883-1940
m. Mary E. Smith
Margaretha (Reta) Boyd Street 1886-1969
m. Frank Lorigan
Henry Bruce Street 1887-1972
m. Norma Dondero
Louise Marie Street c. 1889-1939
m. Clarence Le Roy Olson
Edwin (Ed) Cyrus Street 1891-1972
m. Alice Judson
Clarence Herbert Street 1892-1993
m. Mary Cowley
Anna Gladys Street 1894-1992
m. Leo George Fehlman
George Street 1897-1993
m. 1921 Kathryn (Kay) Alberta Heunisch
m. 1932 and 1938 Nina M. Lenzeva-Nevsorova

George and Kathryn's children:

George (Georgie) Street Jr. 1922-2022
Barbara Jean (Street) Olsen 1924-2012

George Street c. 1909
(George Street Archive)

chapter 1

Words of Wisdom

April 1919
At Sea

Nothing prepared me for the pain when I pierced my tattoo. Electric shocks shot up my arm. I gasped. During all my years on this earth, I have never broken a bone, been to a doctor, or been seriously ill. Hell, I'd never been seasick as I plowed the Pacific for months at a time on the *SS Rose City, Columbia, Alliance,* and *Idaho.*

I clenched my teeth, held my breath, and focused on the blue veins pulsing in my forearm, flaying like I was skinning a fish, timing my cuts to the ship's roll. Inhale. Cut. Exhale. The wooden spoon between my teeth crushed. Blood and pus saturated the towel—and I spit wood splinters and words no mother should hear her son say.

Tears pooled. Sweat dripped into my eyes. I spat out the spoon and grabbed a towel to wipe my face. The smell of my rotting flesh mingling with the scents of oil, tar, musk, and smoke made me gag.

My shipmate grimaced and gripped my arm tighter. I took another swig of whisky and spoon in—continued—reflecting on how I got myself into this mess.

***

"Come on, George, let's celebrate," my fellow radioman had said when we docked in Yokohama the day before on my twenty-second birthday.

"Hey, George is buying," he shouted to the crew before I could speak. "It's his birthday."

Well, one drink led to another, and soon I was in a chair with my shirt sleeve rolled to my elbow, forearm exposed. I was getting a tattoo. As a needle hammered away, my shipmates egged me on. I departed the seedy parlor with a red and blue anchor, sore but proud to have joined the brotherhood of sailors everywhere. Now I wanted to turn back the clock.

When I told Mother I was going to be a radioman on a steam schooner back in 1916, she said, "George, sailors are not the kind of company we usually keep. They do crazy things when drunk, like getting a tattoo."

I hate it when she's right.

Earlier that day in the radio room, I had glanced down to locate the pole that secured my desk to the deck so I could hook my leg around it to keep my chair from rolling. Cramped was a generous word for the space, which also contained my bed. I didn't dare make a move without purpose. My body was a puzzle piece in my workspace crammed with transmitters, receivers, a gimbaled emergency lamp, and an antenna disconnect switch. I even fashioned a shelf for my typewriter—which I bolted down—to create a bit more room. With my arm extended to grasp my chair, I spotted the thin red line slithering like a snake toward my heart.

Worrying over the line, I plugged in and leaned out the porthole for a breath of fresh air with my earphones on just as a flash of lightning lit the sky. A blue spark jumped from my ears to my neck and zapped me like a giant hornet. Sparks hurled around my head. It was not a good day.

I grounded the crystal set's antenna to avoid being blown up by static discharge while I monitored SOS signals in fifteen-minute intervals. New regulations implemented six months after the sinking of *RMS Titanic* required twenty-four-hour watches. That was because a radioman hadn't heard the Titanic's distress calls. He had turned in for the night when his ship was just a couple of miles from the Titanic's position.

My tattoo was sore, red, swollen, and angry; the thin red line had moved two inches by the time my watch ended. It was time to report to the first mate. I dreaded the encounter. He ate crewmen for breakfast. He was a taciturn old salt, chin grizzled with stubble, and his dehydrated face scarred and pocked like a piece of old leather.

"A moment, sir?" I asked.

He took one look at me and barked, "Street, ya look like a drowned rat. What's the matter with ya?"

"I think I have blood poisoning, sir," I said, cradling my arm.

"What makes ya think that? You ever had it before?"

"No, sir. It's just this red line creeping up my arm."

"Well, hell. Now, what have ya gone and done?" He grabbed my elbow and yanked me forward for a closer look. His jaw worked as he chewed his thoughts. He smelled like the ship—rank from dead fish, sawdust, sea salt, and grease. Our ship used to haul fish and supplies to canneries along the Pacific coast. Now she hauled lumber. I got a good whiff of his breath as he bent for a closer look. The stench gagged me.

"Yup, ya got blood poisoning, alright. What ya gonna do about it?" He asked as he stared me down and dared me to whine.

I met his gaze.

"I tried a tincture."

"Well, that's fine and dandy now. Didn't do ya a bit of good, did it. And ya wasted ship stores. You young fellas always think ya knows everything. Tincture. I coulda told ya it wouldn't work. Now, ya've gone an' made it worse. What are ya going to do? There ain't no doctor on board."

"What should I do, sir? I'm asking for your advice. Can we head to port?"

"Who the hell do you think ya are? The Queen of Sheba?" He bellowed. His face turned red, and his eyes drilled into mine. "We don't go to port every time a drunken sot gets hurt. Cut her out, man! Ain't no one gonna do it for ya," he added as he dropped my arm and headed for the deck. "Try not to kill ya 'self. I don't want to do the paperwork. Makes no difference to me if we have a radioman on board. Don't believe in those newfangled contraptions anyway. Go to port he wants. Queenie Street wants us to go to port!"

Queenie Street! I'd never live it down if he called me that in front of the crew. What an ass.

The hatch banged behind the first mate, sucked shut by whipping wind, cutting off the tumult of the storm when he left me to my fate. Spray dampened my shirt. I stared at the wetness and inhaled.

Windber's two hundred horsepower engines could reach ten and a half knots in a pinch, but my condition was not considered a pinch. The first mate had made that clear. There would be no help from that quarter.

After my talk with the first mate, I headed to the radio room, crashing around like a monkey in a cage with each roll. The life preserver hanging on the wall with *SS Windber* stamped on its face flopped and banged into my arm. Rivers of pain shot through my body. The ship shuddered under my feet as a wave barreled over the bow. I fastened myself to the rail by the crook of my good elbow, locked my hands, spread my feet, and waited for the roll to end before I took another step. I used my shoulder to keep my arm from slamming into the bulkhead. The reassuring engine vibrations continued to rumble like a heartbeat, and with my good arm, I grabbed at handholds and made my way to the radio room.

When I had spoken to the first mate, most hands were on deck checking the lines securing the lumber we'd loaded in Bellingham and Seattle. I was pretty sure no one overheard the "Queenie Street" remark. They were concerned about a shift in weight which could be deadly in high seas. One wave could roll the ship belly-up if the center of gravity wasn't just so.

Our bow plunged into a trough. Green water washed the decks. Crewmen dodged the large booms used for hoisting the cargo aboard that rattled and swayed like a couple of praying mantises ready to strike. We were heavy because we'd taken on a full load of coal for our boilers in Honolulu. It was dangerous. My blood poisoning might not need fixing if the crew didn't secure the lines.

When I finally reached the radio room, my relief stared at me and said, "George, are you fit for duty? You look terrible. Did you talk to the first mate?"

"Yes, I'm fine," I replied and plopped into the oak chair.

"You are not fine. Don't ignore this, and hope for the best. What'd the first mate say about returning to port?"

"What do you think he said? I replied. "He sure as hell isn't going to turn this bucket of bolts around in this storm. I'll be fine. I'll take care of it at the end of my watch. Send my Ma a radiogram if I don't make it," I said half-heartily. He was my pinochle partner and one of the sailors who'd egged me on.

So, now here I was, hacking away at my flesh during a gale.[1] Today I added a phrase to my list of sea salt philosophies: "If you want something done, do it yourself."

Before I started my "operation," I had laid a towel on the table so highly painted it was as slick as metal. Then I laced my legs around the bench secured to the table. It was unmovable, and so was I. I pulled out a bottle of whisky.

"Go for it, George," my buddy said as he slapped me on the back. "You better not wait for the storm to abate. Your tattoo looks bad." The overhead light swung back and forth, mimicking the rhythm of the ship, casting gruesome shadows across the mess.

I took a good long swig and poured it over my tattoo.

"Damn it all to hell." I gritted my teeth and took another swig, bracing myself.

"Better have a swig, too. You look kinda green," I said to the mate who had agreed to give me a hand.

He clamped my arm in his meaty hands after taking a good gulp. It was now or never. I huffed and inserted the blade of my sharpened pocket knife into the edge of my tattoo.

My knife couldn't pierce my skin, and the soreness around the area was excruciating. I adjusted the angle like when I cut a tomato, and I still couldn't break the skin.

"Aggg!" A stream of expletives escaped my mouth that made even me blush.

The ship's cook ambled over and said, "Now you're sounding like a real sailor. I bet you don't put those words on your fancy machine. Here, you'll never get it done with that girlie knife. I'll cut," he offered, "and I won't be a pussy about it." His hands were like dog's pads, so calloused that only a deep cut drew blood.

"No, you'd cut my arm off and serve it in a stew. I'll do it," I said through gritted teeth.

He handed me a boning knife that he'd dipped in boiling water. He also gave me a wooden spoon.

"What was the spoon for?" I asked.

"You'll see," he replied. "It'll keep ya from saying words that would make your Ma blush." Then he sat across from me with the look of the devil in his eye. There was no way I'd let him touch my arm. I didn't want to become one of his sea stories.

While I flayed my skin with the spoon securely in my mouth, the cook said, "Now you're gettin' her. You're going to have a helluva scar to show the girls."

His encouragement did not help. Would girls recoil when they saw it? I was a pretty handsome guy up till now.

I removed about a third of the tattoo and cut through to muscle, so I was sure to get all of the infection. The cook poured whiskey on my open wound as his paws clenched my arm. I blew the spoon across the table and let out a howl. The cook's eyes bored into mine—yellowed with age, veined and rough from days of hard living—daring me to whimper.

Never. I'd rather die than show weakness in front of this lot.

My shipmate helped with the bandage and gave me a hearty thump on the back. "No fancy doctor for you; you got it done," he smirked.

Just then, the first mate stepped over the gunwale into the mess.

"Well, now, is Queenie Street whining?" he said to my consternation.

The cook said, "Queenie Street!" and had a good laugh at my expense as he turned back to his stove. I was too sore to care and knew better than to say more.

The first mate said on his way out, "Queenie Street, looks like I won't have to do any paperwork on ya after all. Get some rest. Ya got radio work to do." He was right. I'd live, but I'd never live down Queenie Street. I took another swig of whiskey, returned to my bunk, and curled into the hull. Damn, I should have listened to Ma.

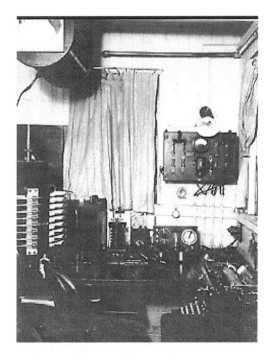

Note on back of photo: "Radio room *SS Columbia* 1916, Marconi receiving set on shelf, Murdock tuning transformer, audiotron detector, amplifying phones."
(George Street Archive)

chapter 2

Into the Ether

1919
Pacific

Nine days had passed since we left Yokohama. Nine days of going on watch and off with constant bandage changes is not easy when blood is stuck to the wrap like a child clinging to its mother. Only a hearty yank separated the two. Gradually, skin supplanted the oozing wound, and I had a helluva scar. The bottom and sides of the tattoo remained — a testament to a memorable night and its consequences.

I was a bit wiser, proud of myself for how I'd handled the tattoo episode. My brother Ed, seven years my senior, had constantly berated me for seeking comfort from Ma when I was injured. "What a baby!" he'd say. "Reta is tougher than you."

It didn't matter to Ed that Reta was ten years older than me. If Reta were around, she'd give Ed a swat, and Ma would patch me up — usually.

***

We steamed to the Philippines, a country as scarred by war as my forearm. Trade had increased fivefold under Colonial America, which was one reason it was a consistent port-of-call. We docked in Iloilo for a load of sugar. A group of us escaped the ship for several hours but not until the first mate had cautioned us with his usual gruff pronouncement, "Stay close to the wharf and don't bring anything back on board that can't be cured with a tincture!"

Transfer Station. *(George Street Achieve)*

"Let's try Filipino food, no matter the consequences," I said to my shipmate. "If I can understand an item on the menu, I'm ordering it."

We headed for Mulle Loney Street, which hugged the waterfront and settled on an outdoor eatery in a thatched-roofed storefront next to a columned warehouse. I ordered chicken Adobo with rice and a soda water. What a delightful change from shipboard fare! We didn't linger long and left with stomachs that didn't rebel.

Our next port of call was Shanghai, a human melting pot of rickety morality and the perfect port for a bunch of sailors too long at sea. We smelled it before we spotted it; there were too many people too close together.

On the 29th of May, we sailed past the two large islands that bisect the mouth of the Yangzi River.[2] Then we turned to port at the mouth of the Huangpu River and steamed its quarter-mile-wide waters to downtown Shanghai. We heaved-to and eased into an empty berth at the Bund. Our metal hull elbowed wooden bumpers that rocked the ship to rest as I leaned over the rail for a better view.

The smell of damp rope, tar, and brackish water took me right back to that pier in Oakland's inner harbor, three and a half blocks from our house. Dad swam it daily to the wet end of Alameda beyond the channel buoys. That's where he heaved me into the bay and told me to swim. I swallowed gallons of estuary water, but, by golly, I learned. I'm still amazed when I run into a sailor who says he cannot swim. What the heck is he doing on a ship?

We had three days to explore the Paris of the East while we took on cargo. The first mate lined us up like a bunch of school kids and said, "You landlubbers ever hear of being shanghaied? They particularly like radiomen, especially young, good-looking ones," he said staring right at me. "If you're not careful, you'll find yourself with more than a sore arm when ya sober up in the bowels of some filthy ship. You stay together. And don't expect me to come looking for ya if you're not here when we leave port. I am not your mother!"

Smirks and snickers escaped the crew.

"Stay in the International and French Settlements," he continued, "They run their own show. China has no power there. Stay away from China City. If you get in trouble, head to the American Consulate on North Yangtze Road. If you're thrown into jail, ya better have money for your bail. I won't pay a yen for the likes of you. Stick with a buddy, and don't come back with the clap," he barked. He gave us fair warning; I planned to stay glued to the sides of my burlier shipmates when I went to a bar.

I slung my camera around my neck, buttoned my wallet into the pocket of my white linen pants, and headed to the Bund with my mates. Distracted by the rumble of rickshaws, the blaring of car horns, and the babel of languages, I almost went ass over tea kettle as I descended the gangway in my new handmade shoes from Yokohama.

"I gotta get pictures of this," I told my mate when we stepped foot on the dock. "Hang on a second." I loaded film into my camera and cranked the first frame forward. Workman loaded goods of all shapes and sizes onto carts. Black-clad men lashed bundles onto bamboo poles and carried them on their shoulders. I set the f-stop, shutter speed, focused, and snapped a picture.

Children next to the Bund, Shanghai c.1919 *(George Street Archive)*

Turning, I captured children playing cards on a scow and a mother rowing her two children.

c. 1919 *(George Street Archive)*

The International District, thick with buildings constructed by wealthy European and American "Shanghai-landers," as they called themselves, reminded me of home. We ignored the concert in the Public Gardens, the Lyceum Theater play, and the nightclubs in first-class hotels. Instead, we headed for the cabarets, brothels, and gambling halls concentrated in a twelve-block area near the racetrack. When we hopped off the trolley, we asked a local, "Women?"

He responded, "You looky women?" and then pointed the way to taxi dancers and female company for a price. One mate in our group said, "You ever done it when you've had a snort of cocaine? It's like it never ends. We gotta get some," and he descended the stairs into the building's basement and an opium drug den. A sticky sweet smell wafted to the sidewalk. I stood in the doorway taking it all in while he purchased and powdered up with snow. Skeletal men stared at me and smiled toothless grins. Their polished eyes shone from a world only they could see, and one I had no desire to experience. I'd learned my lesson about such shenanigans with my tattoo.

"Come on," I said to my mate, who was sniffing from his inhaled whiff of courage. "Let's go to a dance hall. I want to hold a woman in my arms again."

I wasn't new to the business of love. Back in 1917, Marconi assigned me to the *SS Idaho*. I only had a of couple days to visit family before reporting for duty, and the Captain ended up befriending me as we made our way along the California and Washington coast before heading to South America.

Captain Odland got a kick out of me with the earphone cans clamped to my head when he swung by on the way to the bridge. His skin reminded me of a pecan—dark, coarse, and creased, but his blue eyes sparkled like the sea.

"Sparks," that's what most skippers called radiomen, "let me have a listen at them things," he said.

I adjusted the cans as wide as possible to fit across his big Norwegian skull, placed them on his ears, and dialed in the tuner.

"By golly," he said, "it sounds like a bunch of drunks pounding on a table. How the hell can you make sense of that? Is that Morse code? Hey, what are they saying?" He yelled like he was talking to a deaf person. He smacked the earphones back on my head, and I fumbled them in place.

I placed my clipboard on the desktop and began transcribing as rapidly as possible. As words materialized on the paper, the captain said, "By Jiminy, I don't see how you do it. How about if you teach me in exchange for a hand at the wheel?"

I jumped at the opportunity. On my next break, I went to the wheelhouse, and we tackled the basics of navigation. He showed me how to fix on a star to keep on course. Then he joined me in the radio room. I demonstrated how to flip the transmission switch and use the bug.[1] I started him on SOS… dit dit dit, da da da, dit dit dit. His big meaty hand made a mess of it.

Eventually, I took a turn at the helm and practiced keeping old *Idaho* on a steady heading. I was surprised at the strength it took to keep her on course. The ship's weight taxed my muscles and blistered my palms. Sweat slicked my hands and trickled down my brow. I developed a new respect for the watch officers manning the helm. They captained by feel—watching the clouds, sensing the

---

[1] An electromagnetic device for tapping out Morse Code.

movement of the water with their feet, and swaying to the rhythm of the waves.

"Hold her steady," Odland would say, "like a woman pumping away. You gotta love her and guide her with a will. Feel her, George, feel her. She'll let you know what she wants," and he laughed at his own simile while my knuckles turned white.

Cap'n Odland had sailed the seas longer than I'd been alive, long before radio operators like me boarded his ship. Eventually, he preferred to watch me work my radio equipment rather than try it himself. He'd come into the radio room, put on the cans, shake his head like he was trying to rid himself of a swarm of bees, and roar with laughter before smacking my back with his plate-sized hands. "By gol, that's really something ya got there, Sparks," he'd say, almost knocking me off my chair.

Odland also assigned me to "fetch 'em" when we were in port. It was my job to roust his motley crew out of brothels and bars when they overindulged because I was usually the only one who stayed on the north side of sober. When I'd barely got the crew on board in Astoria, Captain Odland yelled, his eyes slippery with alcohol, "Sparks, take the helm. Follow that pilot ship. Everybody's drunk!"[3]

My heart skipped a beat, but I did as commanded. I grabbed the wheel and told the steward, "Make a pot of coffee, NOW! Pour it down the captain's throat if you have to."

The current that hugged the shoreline was like a conveyor belt. Gulls, loons, and seals hitched a ride on it, occasionally diving for food. A seal rolled with ease in the swiftness, its fin creasing the water like a shark's. I did a double take when it tumbled on its back with a flick of its tail, the only bit of him I could see. If I hadn't known better, I would have assumed the seal was a bit of flotsam broken loose from the jetty near Clatsop spit.

When we made it through the churning water at the mouth of the Columbia River just past Fort Stevens, I let out a sigh of relief, thankful for the pilot boat whose wake I followed like a duckling behind its mother.

Shoreline vegetation gave way to a sandy beach as we rounded the south jetty, and the Captain finally took over, sobered up by gallons of coffee. I had made it out of port without incident. And I went up a notch in the eyes of the crew. I wasn't just "Sparks" anymore. Some addressed me by name.

Through my binoculars, I spotted the remains of the *Peter Iredale* that run aground in 1906. It was a constant reminder of the caldron created where the Pacific met the Columbia. Like water and oil, the two did not mix without a good churn.

At the next port of call, the captain bought me more than booze at a brothel to say thank you for a job well done.

"He's a pup, Molly. Show him the ropes," he said when he paid the Madam. He pounded my back and told me, "It's just like being at the helm."

The lady he paid for had a wiggle about her, and I just gawked. My manhood, encouraged by copious amounts of alcohol, overtook my best intentions when she took me by the hand and led me upstairs. My brothers had talked to me about the type of diseases I could get. Actually, they scared the hell out of me.

Unlike Ma, whose vault harbored the mysteries of womanhood and the magical and terrifying ability to birth life, this woman was nameless, a vessel of physical euphoria, nothing more. I reasoned that Mother would never stoop to such baseness. Surely, she and Pa only engaged to procreate.

The moisture of the lady's mouth and the caress of her tongue sent me soaring into the ether, into that invisible space of light and sound that carried away tension and worry and left me awash in wonder. I was breathless. She was faceless. My first experience lasted only moments. Bliss lingered, but drink muddled my memory.

I never mentioned my encounters in my letters to Ma. I was still baffled by girls even though I had three sisters. They were as mysterious as the ether—like whiffles in the wind, as powerful as the radio waves that spanned the oceans, and yet invisible to logic and all rationale. How could a person bleed every month and yet not die? What mysterious power did they hide beneath their skirts? Ma never told me. Pa gave me a talk, but it didn't make a lot of sense. He had said, "You'll learn, don't worry about it. It's all part of growing up."

One thing I knew for sure was that I wanted to "grow up" some more as we made our way to the dance hall.

chapter 3

Wind Tossed

1919
SF Bay Area

After Shanghai, where I had more recreation then rest, we stopped in Honolulu for coal, filled our hull with pineapple products, and then set our course for San Francisco. Heavy, we still made good time as we slapped our way across the Pacific, bouncing off the waves.

Radio traffic didn't pick up until we approached the Farallon Islands, the Devils' Teeth, as the old-timers called them. A lighthouse winked a warning, and the bark of seals told us to steer clear. Though not as romantic as the hula girls in Honolulu, their music was as welcoming, for it meant I was close to home.

The Farallons are more rock than islands, thirty miles west of the mouth of San Francisco Bay. When I was twelve, Teddy Roosevelt designated them as a wildlife refuge because Russian fur traders and egg harvesters had almost wiped out the bird and seal populations.

Now it has hard to distinguish the guano from the seabirds perched precariously onto the cliff faces. The boisterous birds drowned out the sound of breakers. I spotted a whale on my way to the radio room when its water geyser broke the horizon.

I plugged in and chatted with the handful of sailors sheltered in several buildings on the southeast island.

I keyed in Morse code, "QRK" (Do you receive me well?)

"QRX (Your signals are weak.) QRD" (Where are you going?)

I tapped, "QRD Frisco"

A blitz of static interrupted our exchange, and a guy who said he was trying to set up a date with his gal wanted us off the frequency. The closer we got to land, the crazier the radio traffic became since there were no regulations and frequencies were shared. I happily signed off at the end of my watch and went to the deck.

A blanket of wet and frothy mist enveloped us. I tuned in my ears like a wireless and strained my eyes, trying to pierce the veil. I love fog and its grayness. It creates an intimacy, a separateness that shrouds the world. At night, lights blink in swirls, and the mist amplifies sound. Steam whistles, shouts, and the cry of gulls tumble like water into a pool, animating the city lights.

Gray fingers of haze clutched the valleys of the Marin Headlands like an old woman's hand as we approached San Francisco. Fog horns moaned—the further away, the lower the wail.

Guided by a tug past the potato patch of shoals outside the headlands, we steamed into the Bay. The marine layer lifted and descended in pulses and curled back to sea. Alcatraz, Yerba Buena, and Angel Islands remained on our port side as we approached the wharf. A rat scampered down a piling when we drew near. The acrid smell of tar was so intense I tasted it at the back of my throat.

We shuddered to rest, secured lines and dropped the gangplank. I was anxious to regain my land legs, but a stack of messages kept me busy as crew members alerted their families that they had arrived. I sent a radiogram to Ma to let her know I would be home for dinner.

I caught the ferry to Oakland just as the sun set the sky ablaze. Hastily stuffing my duffle under the wooden bench, I stood at the rail to relish the golden light. The crowd and the scent of women cheered my soul. I was in familiar territory again, surrounded by my own kind, comforted by the mental map of my surroundings.

Anxious to tread the pavement of accustomed roads, I jostled my way to the front of the line when we disembarked.

"Pardon me, sir. Excuse me, ma'am." Elbows poked, and eyes glared, but I didn't care. Hurrying across the streets toward home with my bag slung over my shoulder, I skipped up the front steps and flung open the door.

"Ma, I'm home!" I shouted as I tossed my bag on the porch with a thump. She stepped out of the kitchen, threw her arms around my neck, and hugged me as only a mother could. She was lavender, vanilla, beef stew, and home.

Pa ambled over and gave me an enthusiastic handshake. "Welcome home, son," he said, "I want to hear all about your trip. Ma, when's dinner? This young man looks starved."

I recounted most of my adventures over a hearty meal cooked for six but eaten by three. There are details a son never shares with a mother, but over brandy, Pa and I chuckled over my exploits.

"So you're all grown-up now," he said and grinned, shaking his head knowingly.

"I took pictures, Pa, with a camera I bought in Hong Kong. I'll get them developed as soon as I can."

"No surprise. You always loved newfangled things ever since you caused a ruckus in the neighborhood when you built that wireless receiver and transmitter."

After dessert, I fetched the gifts I'd purchased for them—a broach and earrings for Ma, black with silver inlay. For my sisters, I bought black velvet brocade. Pa and my brothers received exotic leather wallets.

Pa offered me a brandy—a first for me. We sat in the front room, sipping and chatting until bedtime. After goodnights all around, I settled in my bedroom. Ma hadn't moved a thing. The wooden dresser drawers cried when I pulled them out, stiff from non-use. Ma lined them with butcher paper, and I put my clean clothes in.

"Ma, I have laundry," I hollered.

"Leave it in the hall, and we'll get it in the morning."

I flopped on my old bed and slept deeply, untroubled, under a roof that didn't rock and shudder from the constant pounding of waves. I was home—and it felt good.

Within days Marconi reassigned me to the *Windber*. I needed a break. I wanted to stop meandering around the planet—to be a Street with an address for a while.

At the next Freemason meeting of Oakland Lodge 188, I shared my desire to become land-based with my mentor, William (Bill) Ryan Sibbett, Jr., older and a member of the Live Oak Lodge.

Marconi had reassigned me to the *Windber* but it was time for me to stop meandering about the planet—to be a street with an address.

"Bill, Ma says it's time for me to settle down, and I couldn't agree more. I'm sick of going to sea." I said. "I've made a land-based request with Marconi, but they assigned me to a ship again. I'm looking for something more."

Sibbett & Street *(Courtesy of Scott Sibbett)*

"My father is talking about expanding his sterilized rag business, he said. "Want me to make inquiries?"

"Sure, it wouldn't hurt. I've got funds stashed away. Let's talk about it."

In July, I had raised the sign on a warehouse in San Lorenzo, "Sibbett & Street Sterilized Wiping Rags." Almost before the paint had dried, our business burned to the ground. Cleaning chemicals and boilers do not mix. My hope of striking it rich on land went up in smoke. Where my dreams once dwelled, tombstones stumps remained.

After Ma rustled up a breakfast of fresh eggs, bacon, and homemade bread, I headed downtown to get my photographs developed. My brother Clarence and his wife lived in a boarding house in Alameda, and he'd invited me to dinner that evening. I hoped to have some pictures to show them.

"George, come to dinner," he'd said. "I want to get a look at you and hear all about your adventures in the Orient and your 'business.'" It had been a while since I'd seen him. My chest had filled out, and

I'd grown a mustache. My newly tailored suits accommodated my beefier size—no more hand-me-downs for me.

Kay sitting between her mother and sister. *(George Street Archive)*

When I arrived at the boarding house behind Alameda High School on 2224 San Antonio Avenue with gifts in hand, a blond, blue-eyed beauty answered the door. "Nice to meet cha," she quipped as she gestured me in.

"Didn't I see you at a bus stop?"[4]

"Yes. I called you Clark Gable."

"You did. And I called you Lillian Gish."

"I'm Kathryn, Kathryn Heunisch with a 'sch' at the end," she said through pursed lips, "but you can call me Kay. My mother runs the boarding house, and I help out. So does my sister."

"Nice to see you, again—Kay. I'm looking for my brother Clarence. He invited me to dinner."

"Oh, I know. We've made a good old American meal for you—fried chicken."

"Thank you. I always look forward to home cooking." She swung away, leaving a trail of vanilla in her wake. Shalimar perfume, perhaps.

Clarence sauntered over.

"Hi, Clarence," I said as I pumped his hand.

Turning to Kay, I said, "He is one of my *older* brothers, married to Mary, the lady in the blue dress standing by the window."

"I know that," Kay said, causing me to blush to my toes. "They are going to be moving out of this hen house soon. Their new house is almost finished."

We laughed, and Mary joined us. She said, "Yes, we'll be out in a couple of weeks. Come, let's sit down for dinner." Mary took Clarence's arm.

When we were seated with Kay on my right, Kay asked, "Did you go to school in Alameda?"

"No, I went to Cole Grammar School, then Oakland Polytech. We live on Magnolia Street off Market."

Clarence said, "Remember when we passed out the Emeryville racetrack dope sheets after our paper routes?"

"That was a gas." I said.

"What's a dope sheet?" Kay asked.

"It's a listing of the horses racing at Emeryville the next day. We posted them in the local bars along Peralta, Webster and 7th Street—the saloons near the steam train terminals."

Clarence said, "I'd tell George to grab the food intended for the patrons while I pasted the sheet to bulletin board. By the time we got home we had our newspaper sacks filled with crackers, cold cuts, cheese, pretzels, and slices of bread—you name it."[5]

"I gave our snatchings to Ma after Clarence and I filled our bellies."

We had a grand time sharing our remembered antics while Kay flitted and fluttered about like a butterfly. She acted as hostess and entertained us with her Ouija Board after dinner. Her beauty took my breath away. She was slim, with a pert, turned-up nose, and wore her hair in a stylish bob. And boy, what a flirt. She coyly glimpsed over her shoulder when her skirt caught in the door and exposed her calf. I couldn't take my eyes off her. I got lost in the pools of her blue eyes as she pouted, stroked her hair, and posed in a Tallulah Bankhead sort of way. How she hadn't been snapped up by now was beyond me.

"Wow," I said to Clarence. "I think I just found the reason to leave my seafaring life behind." I was pretty sure Kay was within hearing distance—I hoped she was. She turned her head and glanced in my direction. I did want more of that.

"Mrs. Heunisch?" I asked when it was time for me to leave. "May I make an appointment with your husband? I want to ask permission to step out with Kay."

"Mr. Heunisch is not part of this family," she responded. "We divorced when Kay was little."

"Oh, well then, I'll ask you. May I call upon Kay?"

"Yes, you may," Mrs. Heunisch said. "I expect you to be gentlemanly at all times."

I made arrangements for the next afternoon and thanked Mrs. Heunisch for the best dinner I'd ever had, even though I couldn't remember what we'd eaten.

Clarence walked me to the door.

"Well, how about that?" he said. "It looks like Georgie Porgie has found his puddin' and pie."

I hated being called Georgie Porgie. At my twelfth birthday party, my pals teased me because I wore short pants.[6] I was too old for knickers and stockings, but hand-me-downs were my only clothes. They chanted, "Georgie Porgie puddin' and pie, kissed the girls, and made them cry. When the boys came out to play, George Porgie ran away."

I remember snapping, "I'm not Georgie Porgie. I'm a Street, not a Porgie, a road, boulevard, or highway. I'm a Street—and of course, the others laughed and continued teasing.

"Clarence, it appears you had more in mind for me than just dinner," I said ignoring his tease.

"Kay is a beauty, that's for sure."

"Her family has had tough times. I don't know the details, but you need to dig into that before going further," he cautioned. "You don't want to bite off more than you can chew."

Brotherly advice. Clarence was married. What did he know? I'd seen more of the world than he ever would.

I told Clarence, "I don't give a hoot about her family troubles. She is as different from Ma and my sisters as rough water from still. I want her."

"Well, don't jump overboard before you get in too deep," he said as he closed the door behind me.

I had to walkup Walnut to Santa Clara to catch the streetcar for the ride home. My stomach and heart were full. I think most men experience a deep, innate drive to procreate, to leave a living legacy so they will not be forgotten. The urge came over me in waves, crashing my psyche like breakers over the bow, creating a storm of desire perpetrated by a glance. After meeting Kay, I was like a wind-tossed ship plunging into a trough, startled by my reaction and embarrassed by my wooden response. When I got to the street, I glanced back and spotted Kay at the window, leaning seductively against the frame, and the wave washed over me again.

***

Ma assembled the clan and a handful of acquaintances for a holiday dinner the following weekend. It was December already and I was still adrift, living at Ma's, and reluctant to head to sea. Clarence and Mary brought Kay. She caught my eye when they walked in, cocked her head, and gave me the once-over. I think I passed inspection.

She spotted my botched tattoo when I rolled up my sleeve to show off my tattoo to my brothers. Braided scar tissue laced my forearm, and what was left of my anchor was just recognizable.

Ma took one look and said, "George, why did you go and do a stupid thing like that? You never listen to me. I told you men get into trouble when they drink. Now, look at what you've gone and done to yourself." Ma was not happy, and when Ma was not happy, nobody was happy.

"Georgie Porgie, you blockhead. You deserve what you got," my brother Ed said. My sister Reta rolled her eyes and called me foolish. I'd endured my shipmate's guffaws, and now this. I regretted showing off my mistake.

Sensing my distress, Kathryn came to my side and lightly ran her fingers back and forth over my scar. A tingle raced up my arm.

"My mother rubs my arm like this to help me sleep," she said. "It always sooths me." She cocked her head but kept her eyes on mine. Kay's skin was flawless. Memories of my explorations in Japan's *Yukaku* (red-light district*)* flashed through my mind. All I had to do then was point to a girl, then the picture of the act I wanted to be performed, pay the Mama-san, and well…it was legal, indulgent, and satisfying. I brushed aside the memories before I made a bigger fool of myself.

"Kay, you are fortunate to have such a comforting mother," I said as I rolled my sleeve over my badge of honor.

***

After two teas at her house, Kay's mother agreed to let me take her out on a chaperoned date. I went in for a full-court press, just like when I was the high school basketball team captain.

Kay said with delight, "I just love to dance."

I took Kay and her older sister, Bessie, to lunch in Chinatown, where we had our names inscribed in Chinese on red paper banners. I bought Kay a wooden mouse figurine while window shopping.

"For luck," she said as she slipped it in her pocket.

Later in the week, we went to the Grand Lake Theater and sat in the front row. We dined at the Claremont in the Berkeley hills and enjoyed picnics at Lake Merritt, lounging among the drooping limbs of the oak trees while Kay's skirt draped teasingly toward the ground. Long walks around the lake took us through the Pagoda where she'd pose like royalty.

"I'm Kathryn of Alameda," she'd say, "namesake of Catherine of Aragon." I bent a knee and kissed her hand. Her vanity beguiled me.

Other times, Kay darted among the redwoods in Tilden Park, daring me to kiss her before Bessie caught up. When I held her, she responded with vim and vigor, frustrating my manhood.

"I like my men tall, dark, and handsome," she said, then batted her eyes and ask, "Would you—for a big red apple?"

"Would I what?" I asked.

"You know," she teased.

Fortunately, Bessie appeared, saving me from making a bigger fool of myself over this woman who drove me wild with desire.

There was no way I would head out to sea again and leave this vixen for others. I had to make her mine. Her mother approved of the upscale establishments I took her to, and she made it clear her daughter was a beauty and only deserved the best. She valued Kay like a rare commodity, and so did a lot of other men, myself included.

I declined Marconi's next sea assignment as Ma continued to nag, "George, It's time you settled down. Your brothers and sisters have started respectable families. It's time you did, too. Life is short."

Ma was right. Banging around in ships and brothels left a lot to be desired. I was an "old salt" now, with a scar to prove it. I'd seen a big chunk of the world's oceans—smelled it, lived it on from Hong Kong to South America, and almost drowned in it in 1917 when I was on the *SS. Serapis*, an ex-German ship interned during the Great War.

We had docked at Lahaina, Maui, to load raw sugar for the East Coast when I made wireless contact with Cebert Capwell. His father—or great-grandfather—founded the original Capwell's store in downtown Oakland. Cebert and I had first connected by wireless in 1912 or so. His amateur station was 6CE or 6CC—can't remember which.

He and Ed Mair, another old wireless friend, worked at the Mutual Telegraph Coy's Lahaina station operated by the U.S. Naval Radio Service when we connected. They got permission to come to my ship, and I was allowed to join them for an afternoon of sailing. We were two to three miles from Lahaina—with me handling the sails—when we shipwrecked. Ed and Cebert had not leaned outboard far enough, our canoe went belly up. As hard as we tried, we could not right her. We ditched our shoes and most of our clothes so we wouldn't be weighed down. Since the upside-down canoe could only support one person at a time, we took turns swimming and resting as we made our way to shore. Once we got into the large breakers at the shoreline, I volunteered to ride the canoe like a surfboard to land. Well, the mast hit bottom, and the hollowed-out log canoe split end to end. We all lived to tell the tale, and that was my one and only shipwreck.[7]

***

A recent visit from my best friend, Frank Muller, and my remembered "shipwreck" made me rethink my path in life.

Muller and I had crewed together on the *SS Serapis* (renamed *SS Osage*). He probably would have joined our sailing misadventure but he was on duty. When we arrived in New York via the Panama Canal, the Navy requisitioned our ship, and offered me and Frank jobs as Second Class Radiomen. Frank accepted their offer. I wanted to hold out for first class, so I bought a ticket on the overland train to Oakland and watched America roll past my window like a motion picture.

Unfortunately, the Navy assigned Frank to *USS Ticonderoga*. A German U-boat sank the ship within days of his departure.

I had no idea Frank had survived until he showed up at my doorstep with a tin of German black bread he had saved for me. I was never so happy to see anyone in my life! He explained that the U-boat surfaced next to him and two others and took them on board because they were officers. They held them prisoner until the end of the war. The rest of the crew and their cargo of horses went to the bottom of the sea.

"What have you been up to, George?" he asked after he finished telling me about his last couple of years.

"There were no land-based radio assignments available when I got back to Oakland, so I took a job at the Southern Pacific Railroad mole—anything to stay off of a ship for a while."

"The mole?"

"That's what we call the combined train station and ferry terminal that fingers its way into the Bay. It divides the Middle Harbor from the Inner Harbor. The view was great."

"How was the job?"

"I lasted a month. It was hot, dirty, mindless work. The only helpful thing I learned was the importance of having a good timepiece."

"What then? Were you still living at home while I was in prison?"

"Yes. Ma insisted. After SP, I got a great opportunity.I taught radio navigation and interception to aviators at the US Army's School of Military Aeronautics at the University of California, Berkeley, for the rest of the war."

"You lucky dog!"

"Yeah, I was. I really appreciated the job. My students' life expectancies, once they took to the air, were measured in weeks instead of years."

"Professor Street," they'd say to me…

"Professor? Do I have to call you Professor now?" he smirked.

"No, of course not. 'Professor,' they'd say, 'I'm off to punch holes in those clouds, to fly through those valleys and mountains of air, to blast a Hun from the sky.' I didn't expect to see them again. After the war, the Aeronautics school closed; I'd had no choice but to return to American Marconi."

Ma entered the parlor and announced that Muller was to stay for dinner. "I want to put some meat on your bones," she told Muller. "You boys catch up. You've got a whole new life ahead of you."

How could he refuse? Ma was right. We had a lot to talk about—past, present, and future. I wanted to tell him about Kay.

chapter 4

"I will wait for you."

1920
SF Bay Area

Kay not only created a pinch in my pants, but she also put a crimp in my funds. She was not a cheap date. When I asked if I could call on her, I had no idea I would be standing in line. It was not unusual for her to go out three times a week. One weekend she went to the same county fair on four separate occasions with four different guys, returning with trinkets and baubles purchased or won in an attempt to buy her favors. I'd given Kay Japanese silk, Chinese incense, and a copper bracelet from South America—gifts from real places, not knock-offs purchased at a fair. I hoped they gave me an exotic edge over my competition. She wore the bracelet I gave her constantly, extending and wiggling her hand to let the world know she had captured the attention of a worldly man and not just a local boy.

Her mother was askance at the attention she was receiving, fearful of losing her to the ravages of sin. My mother hoped she was a passing fancy. Kay had cast off her Victorian dress and corset for free-flowing, dropped waist shifts draped with long beaded necklaces or a boas. She painted her flawless skin with rouge, arched her brows, and reddened her lips. She was a "flapper" who wanted to roar in the Twenties.

Ma asked, "How could someone like her ever settle down and raise a family?"

I replied defensively, "How could she not? She's a woman, isn't she? We make a striking couple and will have beautiful children. You're just being old-fashioned."

Within days of my request for a land-based assignment, Marconi of America assigned me to the receiving station in Marshall, California, just north of Point Reyes. It was far enough away from the massive transmitter in Bolinas so the spark crashes would not drown out the signals we were trying to hear.[8] More importantly, it was close enough to the Bay Area so that I could return during my time off.

I was cold and miserable at this fog-shrouded station, and Kathryn haunted my dreams. The scent of her Shalimar perfume lingered on my skin for the first couple of days. I sent her telegrams so she wouldn't forget me and succumb to the attentions of others.

When I completed the Marshall job, Marconi assigned me to a civilian post with the Navy at their Yerba Buena Island keying station on the San Francisco-Pearl Harbor NPG/NPM circuit. The old-timers called Yerba Buena, "Goat Island," because gold rush squatters had released goats to browse its hills. Four landline circuits connected

Goat Island to Mare Island for arc and spark control, transmission, and other apparatus operations.[9]

When I arrived at the station, I walked into a five-foot-high stack of commercial messages bound for Japan in English and Romaji, Romanized Japanese. Follow-up messages poured in. I emptied my mind, focused on the letters, and pounded my mechanical key for hours, converting letters to dots and dashes as fast as humanly possible so I could finish and see Kay again.

"How about a picnic at my station?" I asked Kay during my next day off. I'd gone straight to her house because she had complained about not seeing enough of me.

"Oh, I'd love that. I'll make fried chicken."

Her mother stepped in. "Will you be alone? I won't allow it unless there are others with you."

"There are people all over the island, Ma'am," I reassured her. "There are other radiomen in the shack since it is manned around the clock. And there are goat herders and tourists. The views are spectacular."

With her mother's blessing, we hopped on the ferry at the mole. Kay's hair blew across my face as we hugged the rail. The picnic basket at our feet and the smell of fried chicken made my stomach growl.

"Are you growling at me?" Kay asked.

I made some pithy remark and gave her a kiss, accidently bumping against her as we docked. After we jostled our way to the pier, we climbed aboard the open-air, six-passenger jitney for the ride up the hill to the station.

We set the picnic basket on the table, and I gave her a tour of the building. Equipment covered the shiplap siding and just about every level surface. I didn't show her our living area because the man on night shift was sleeping.

We picnicked in the screened porch area, which had commanding views of the bay. Sausalito and Tiburon ferries streamed through wisps of fog. Alcatraz's military disciplinary cell block and lighthouse loomed within spitting distance of us. Angel Island, the Ellis Island of San Francisco, had only a whisper of life at the Immigration Center.

"Look, there's a ship just like my first, *SS Alliance*," I pointed out to Kay. "She was a bucket of bolts, but she was my first rust bucket, and I loved the old girl."

"Why do you refer to the ship as a girl?" Kay asked.

"In the U.S., ships are females. In Germany, they are males."

"I've never heard of such a thing."

"Sailors love their ship just like they love their women and mom."

"Sounds like they'd been at sea too long."

"Yes, I love being at sea but long for home, too. Life is not as complicated at sea, and there is only so much to do."

"What did you do all day?"

"I sat at my desk in the radio room with headphones clapped to my head listening for pulses in the ether. I turned the tuner dial until the Morse code signals registered clearly before flipping the transmit switch to reply."

"How boring."

I laughed. "I felt like a peeping tom. In my half-sleep, I translated, unable to let go of the rhythm of the dots and dashes. Now I dream about you."

Kay smiled and cocked her head, obviously pleased to hear that she was on my mind.

"Was your Ma okay with you going off to sea?"

"No. She was beside herself. None of my brothers had gone. I took Ma and Pa to tour the ship. I needed their permission since I was only eighteen. Dad took a picture of Ma and me beside the main smoke stack. I put my arm across her shoulders, hoping to reassure her, but she remained dour as she stood there in black. Pa signed for me, telling Ma, "It's time, Mother. It's time for George to see the world and become a man.""

"Well, I can reassure him that you are *all* man."

By the time we headed home, I had lipstick on my collar.

At the end of 1919, I feared for my job when General Electric acquired Marconi Wireless Telegraph Company of America (American Marconi). When the Great War broke out, the government had taken over American Marconi because of security concerns. When it ended, and it was time to return communications

George Street and his mother C.1916
(George Street Archive)

companies to private status, Assistant Secretary of the Navy, Franklin D. Roosevelt, wanted American wireless to be American-owned. So, he facilitated an acquisition of American Marconi by General Electric, the patent holder for the Alexanderson high-frequency alternator needed for long-distance transmission. G.E then formed Radio Corporation of America (RCA) to run wireless operations.[10]

G.E. bought everything—all the capital, debt, technology, and human assets, including me. The commercial manager of American Marconi, David Sarnoff, a Russian immigrant, was also part of the deal. He moved to RCA in the same capacity.

I related to Sarnoff. At the age of nine he had sold newspapers to help support his family, just as I had done. However, at the age of thirteen, he became the sole supporter when his father took ill.[11] Two years later, Sarnoff walked into his destiny. He mistook a telegraph office for a newspaper office and without a second thought became a "Coni man," working as a messenger while learning the trade. By the time Sarnoff was thirty, he was General Manager of RCA and a very rich man.

I was on my way up too. RCA tapped me for Radio Supervisor at the Koko Head Station in Honolulu. My familiarity with Hawaii from my seafaring days made me the perfect candidate. I had finished transmitting the great pile-up of delayed messages at Goat Island. Staying was a dead-end. I could never afford Kay on an operator's salary.

I desperately wanted to take the position. They were offering me the opportunity to work in the land of my dreams. I had first connected to Koko Head when I was thirteen, while building and rebuilding various tuner-coil crystal wireless receiving sets. After finishing my paper route and homework, I helped Ralph Hyde test his handmade six-inch-long, three-filament Audions he was developing for Haller & Cunningham. Several nights a week, we tested two-filament Audions using makeshift flashlight batteries as our "B" voltage supply.

Ralph was an expert glass blower at Oakland Lamp Works and a supervisor at G.E. lamp factory.[12] We encased the filament, plate, and grid in a glass envelope and then evacuated the tube, as they did in lamp construction.

When we established contact, Ralph said, "The tested tubes were considered good if the deep modulating 220 cycle tone of VAE, 900 miles to the north on Vancouver Island, could be heard, and excellent if KHK could be picked up from Honolulu, 2100 miles from

Oakland."[13] All I could think of was that we were connecting to a tropical island paradise through the ether.

Koko Head. Honolulu. Surely, Kay would understand. My pay as supervisor would be $150.00 a month plus room and board.

I went to talk to her—by now we were pretty serious. Anxiety gripped me when she answered the door.

"What is it, George? Cat got your tongue?" she asked when she saw the look on my face.

We locked eyes, and she grabbed my arms. Before her mother walked in, I pulled her to me, kissed her hair, inhaling her scent. She was not making this easy for me.

Pushing her to arm's length I got right to my rehearsed speech. I'd practiced what I was going to say in a weak attempt to settle my nerves.

"Kay, I have been offered a wonderful opportunity that will be sufficient for us to start a life together. You know that is what I want. I feel you want the same. The only problem is that the job is in Hawaii, in Honolulu." I blurted it out before she could say anything because I was sure there would be crying.

She didn't disappoint.

"George, NO! We will never see each other again. I don't even know where Hawaii is. How could you do this to me?" she huddled to my chest as her mother entered the room.

"What is going on?" Mrs. Heunisch bawled. "You, George Street, are being way too familiar with my daughter! Kay, sit down!"

She flopped on the settee, exposing her legs. Her mother glared and Kay tugged her skirt in place.

God, what a tease!

"Mother," Kay said, "George has decided his job is more important than me. He's accepted a position in Lulu something, wherever that is."

Then Kay's vanity kicked in. She wiped her eyes and stuck her nose into the air before turning away from me and my pleading eyes.

I stepped forward, "Mrs. Heunisch, may I explain?" I told her about my RCA opportunity. "I won't expect Kay to wait for me," I added. But secretly, I hoped she would.

I turned to Kay, my heart in my throat, and said, "I will be able to take leave and return stateside to see you. I plan to ask for your hand in a year's time if you are still willing. Once I have secured a suitable house, I will send for you and your mother, and we can wed. You will love Hawaii." Hoping to pique her interest, I added, "There are exotic flowers, beaches, clubs, and theaters. You will want for nothing,"

Her teary eyes gripped mine as though to say, "See what you will miss."

Her mother jumped in. "It's a sensible plan, Kay. It's obvious you have feelings for each other. George has a good head on his shoulders, and he is a gentleman. I think you should wait, Kay, and stop your fooling around."

I had Mrs. Heunisch's support! She approved of me. I glanced at Kay.

She wailed, "What? Am I supposed to live like a nun while you have all the fun?"

"Kay, I'm serious. I love you. Wait for me." My boldness in saying those words in front of her mother shocked even me.

Kay turned her back to me with a "Humph."

"May I call tomorrow?" I asked her mother in a rush of embarrassment and fear, hoping that Kay would come around. "I want to take Kay dancing one last time before I leave."

"What makes you think I want to go out with you? You are leaving me."

"Kay, please," her mother interjected. "Come over, George. I will have a talk with her."

The next day, I arrived at Kay's doorstep with a bouquet of red roses and a sapphire pendant encircled with diamonds. I fastened it around her neck, caressing her skin with my fingers as I did so. I planned to take her to the *Carter and His New Magic Show* matinee —fortune-tellers and magic thrilled her. I wanted to lavish her on our last night together no matter the cost, so I rented a car. Aboard the ferry, we fogged the windows.

After exiting the ferry, we went to the matinee, and then drove up Market to the New Palace Hotel. Tipping the valet, we wove our way through the marble columns to the Garden Room. Kay had draped a boa around her neck and flaunted a cigarette holder. She didn't smoke; her mother wouldn't allow it, so her holder held an unlit one. I'd reserved a screened table hidden behind a lattice divider braced with potted palms. Jewel-like light bounced across the chandeliered room. And the sparkle of Kay's necklace reflected in her eyes. She was stunning.

Men four tables away turned to watch her. Some rotated in their chairs and openly stared. She coyly acknowledged them with a nod of her head and a flip of her boa. When the maître d' seated her, she rested her hand on my shoulder as though to say, "I'm his," and my ego soared.

After dinner, I took her to the Pied Piper Bar upstairs for dancing—and a drink. I'd slipped a flask in my pocket to add a splash of "giggle water" to our Coca-Colas. Prohibition ruled. Most bartenders looked the other way if you brought your own booze.

"Oh George, you're such an evil boy," she said with a smile when I spiked her Coke. She took a drink, and then I grabbed her hand and led her to the dance floor.

"Let's show the world what you've got," I said, feeling like the richest man in the room.

We swept across the room for the audience of envious eyes. With my hand on Kay's bare back, she pressed into my shoulder. Sparks arced between us as bright as the ones in an Audion.

From there, we hopped the cable car to the Fairmont Hotel on Nob Hill. Luxurious and elegant, Kay loved it. She flirted with the rich and famous from across the room, her cigarette holder pointed skyward. I didn't mind because tonight she was mine.

Our last stop to cap our glittering night was for a cup of coffee at Fisherman's Wharf's Buena Vista Café. Fog enveloped us. The city lights misted. We were secluded and silent.

Kay huddled next to me as we walked back to the car. I wrapped the flap of my overcoat around her and pulled her tight. She twisted toward me, and I molded my body to hers so that I could remember every curve. She moaned and teased me with her eyes, measuring my desire—and my integrity. Cupping her face, I kissed her lips and said, "I love you," hoping the words locked into her heart.

"I love you too," she breathed, "I will wait for you. There will be no other."

I pulled away, determined to give her nothing to complain about to her mother, whose boundaries I'm sure I'd crossed.

When we were at her doorstep, Kay said in perfect Lillian Gish style, "Thank you for the marvelous evening, darling." And she lifted her lips to mine. Our parting kiss was passionate and deep and lingering. I wanted to consume this gem of a woman that other men lusted after, no matter the cost.

"I will be back for you soon," I said and I left her standing alone in a pool of light softened by mist.

The next day I steamed to Honolulu—this time as a passenger. As we slipped from San Francisco Bay into the Pacific, I glanced over my shoulder at Alameda, where Kay waited.

My crossing was uneventful and indulgent. I spent time writing to Kay, reading, and visiting the radio room. Single women gave me the eye, but I would have none of it. I jotted in my log: "March 9, 1920. Arrived Honolulu to work at high power radio station at Koko Head."

My next entry read: "April 9, 1920, 23 years old today." Had it been a year since I wrote Mother about Kobe and Yokohama and the hundreds of sampans in the Inland Sea?

***

Down in the dumps because no letter had arrived, Kay and her sister, Bessie, went shopping at the H. C. Capwell Co. department store with money saved from assisting at the boarding house. Her mother had opened their home after the 1906 earthquake and found it an excellent way to earn money. Kay, seven at the time of the big one, remembered the crumbled chimneys, cracked sidewalks, and the sea of smoke on the horizon. Even though they lived in Alameda, their Victorian home rocked and bucked like a ship in a gale. Her mother braced herself in a doorway and screamed to Kay and her sisters to do the same. They stood wide-eyed with fright and straddled the floor like sailors trying to get their sea legs. When the shaking stopped, and the earth became rock-solid again, they ran outdoors to find comfort in familiar faces, not daring to reenter until city inspectors checked the gas lines.

As a consequence of her remembered terror of the 1906 earthquake, the street car ride over the bridge to Oakland frightened her.

"Bessie, what if there's an earthquake when we're on the bridge?"

"Take my hand. We'll be fine," Bessie said. Kay held her breath and exhaled when they finally crossed to the Oakland side and onto Webster Street, grateful they'd made it over without plunging into the water.[14]

When they hopped off the streetcar, they went straight to the millinery sale in Capwell's basement.

"George loves hats." Kay said. "He told me he worked at *Money Back Smith's Men's Haberdashery and Clothing Store* when he was in high school."

"He does dress smartly," replied Bessie.

"That is one of things I like about him. I'm going to buy Andrea hat. He'll like that. It's the latest fashion."

"That should cheer you up."

"Let's stop and buy some Gouraud's Oriental Face Cream on the way to movies."

"It's expanse. You don't need face cream."

"I need to stay beautiful for George. I don't want to look like an old maid when he comes back."

"You will never be an old maid, Kay. Come on, let's not be late for the movie. Mom wants you to pay attention to its lesson."

Their mother had given them an extra quarter to see *Young Mrs. Winthrop* at the Franklin. She told them, "The *Tribune* said it's about a jazz-mad housewife unwilling to give up her happiness for her business-absorbed husband."

Kay did learn a lesson from the film but not the one her mother had hoped for.

chapter 5

Paradise Found

1920
Honolulu, Territory of Hawaii

Needles of light bounced on the sea's surface as our ship eased into the world of greens and blues that is Honolulu. I hugged the rail; my hat pushed back on my head. I turned my face into the wind to relish the warm caress of the offshore breeze once again. I leaned forward to see the activity on the dock. Squinting against the sunlight, welcoming musicians plunked on their ukuleles, and hula girls swayed. I grinned from ear to ear. I was back in my place of fond memories.

Vanilla-sweet whiffs of oleander greeted me as I stepped off the gangway. I walked the short distance to my hotel to get my land legs back. There were more motorcars and Europeans than when I'd last stopped over. Honolulu was growing up, which would help Kay feel more at home.

I settled into a moldy hotel wanting to save as much money as possible for Kay. The hotel was clean enough, cheap, and within easy walking distance of RCA's office on Fort Street.

Within days of reporting for work, I realized I'd stepped into a mess. The five small inter-island spark stations struggled to transition back into private ownership after being taken over by the government during the Great War. I read U. S. Navy Lieutenant Raguet's speech given at the Chamber of Commerce Territorial Committee meeting in August of 1919. He expressed doubts about returning communications to the private sector.[15] It was my job to prove him wrong.

The station at Kahuku had been under American Marconi until the U.S. took control. About five thousand words per day were transmitted on its transpacific circuit because the Navy had ceased sending commercial traffic to Japan and the West Coast. [16]

Kahuku operated as a simplex station due to the low amount of traffic—while a message was being transmitted, an incoming one could not be received, and visa-versa. It needed Alexanderson alternators to fix the problem.[17]

George Street (left) and buddy
next to Chalmers roadster
(George Street Archive)

The receiving station at Koko Head, which had cost the company $400,000, had never been used because of Kahuku's signal interference. Getting Koko Head up and running for commercial use fell to me. My tasks as radio supervisor included upgrading the operating circuits because Oahu's location was important for communication with ships at sea. With help, I installed an antenna atop the 1200-foot-high Koko Crater greatly improving long-distance transmission. Koko Head's steep conical flanks made for a tough climb, but the view was spectacular. I could see Diamond Head from the top. My buddy snapped my picture while I climbed the lattice girders and hammed for the camera, barefoot and swinging from one arm like an ape. Opening the communication links from San Francisco to Hawaii and Hawaii to Japan took a month.

The streets and bridges out Koko Head way were really something. At first, I drove a Chalmers roadster, but I'd get stuck in the mud after two or three days of heavy rains. When we hit that muck, the car danced like roller skates on a polished floor.[18] I would have to wait until it hardened to dig out. I'd roughed

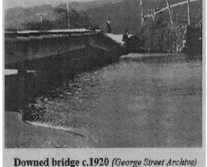

Downned bridge c.1920 *(George Street Archive)*

it overnight more than once under heavy mosquito netting before I finally settled on a good old Harley-Davidson motorbike for transportation. Even then, it took two to four hours to make the ten-mile journey to work when it rained. If a Kona storm blew through, I had to drag the bike by sheer strength up the slopes of washed-out bridges that spanned the fish ponds. Rotted planks exposed nail spikes and blew my tires. Some determined person had placed three boards abreast over the deep sand on the Wai'alae road —which helped—as long as a car hadn't spun out and dislodged them.[19] During high tides, at Maunalua Bay, I'd have to wait for the waves to recede before plowing through the remaining foot of seawater to continue on my way. Sweat, mud, and sea spray covered me from head to toe by the time I arrived. My eyes glowed red if I forgot my goggles.

Eventually, RCA built a thirty-five-room residence hall near the station so we could stay overnight when on duty. Five bedrooms were permanently occupied. The recreation room included a pool table and a player piano, so we organized a dance for about fifty people.[20] We made quite the racket when Marty played the saxophone, Wally strummed the steel guitar, and I banged pie plates for the percussion section.[21] It was a good thing we were isolated.

For our next party, we hired a jazz band from Honolulu. They had a banjo, banjo-guitar, and the whole shebang. As Master of Ceremonies, I helped judge the worst and best dancers. The ladies won a toy snake that shimmied like the best of them.[22]

On my off days, I explored Honolulu and the countryside dreaming about where I would take Kay after we wed. Native Hawaiians and immigrants from China, Japan, the Philippines, and Europe jam-packed the city. In Chinatown, I stumbled upon a wedding reception drawn there by a tremendous racket of music.

RCA Residence Hall (*George Street Archives*)

"Hey, hey, young men, you cummie in and join the party," a Chinese man said as he waved and grabbed my friend's arm. "Good luck for bride and groom for strangers at party, you cummie in." We happily complied and entered a large room festooned with red decorations and packed with people.[23] The sweet smell of Chinese five-spice took me right back to Shanghai. Exotic, colorful, and loud. Kay would have loved it.

Kay and I continued our courtship by telegram and mail. She sent me kisses. Red lipstick prints smeared the paper and dabbled perfume reminded me of her. She also sent her picture. She flirted with the camera, coyly inclining her head sideways and glancing out the corner of her eye. Her hemline was higher than her mother's ever would have been. That was my Kay.

***

On my first visit home, I dropped my duffle on Ma's porch without saying "Hi," and headed to Kay's house. When I arrived at the boarding house, Kay flung open the door and pulled me in. I planted a long, hungry kiss on her lips.

Her mother called, "Kay, who's at the door?"

"It's George!" Kay replied as we pulled apart.

"Let's have tea." Her mother said, "I want to hear all about Hawaii. Kay, give me a hand," she added as she headed to the kitchen. Kay's mother knew better than to leave her alone with a man, as much for the man's sake as for Kay's.

Mrs. Heunisch returned carrying the tea service and poured. Kay took a sip from a cup with a handle shaped like a dragon. Nymphs danced around the outside edge, naked except for wisps of cloth. My mother would have buried the cup on a shelf even though it depicted a Renaissance scene.[24] I couldn't help but wonder if Kay thought it risqué.

I asked, "Have you or your family ever been to Hawaii?"

"No," Mrs. Heunisch replied. Our ancestors migrated from Europe via the East Coast. We dropped the "von" from our name shortly before the Great War ended. As you can imagine, being an American of German heritage was difficult. Kay is second generation American, through and through."

"Yes," Kay piped up, "I went to school in Seattle and Haight School in Alameda."

"I'd love to learn more about the family, I said. Bessie is a dark-headed beauty, as different from Kay as water is to wine."

Mrs. Heuisch replied, "Bessie took after her father. She is engaged to be married now. I will lose her help when she moves to Seattle with her new husband. Kay, go get your sister for tea."

"Doesn't Kay have another sister, Ella?" I asked when Kay left the parlor. "I've heard the name."

Every time I asked Kay about her family, she changed the subject. All I knew was that there were three girls, Ella, Bessie, and Kay. I admit I was probing.

Mrs. Heunisch sighed and dropped her head. She gathered herself and said with a sigh. "Ella died in childbirth a bit over a year ago." She was my first child, a delight to us all." Her voice broke, but she continued. "She was like a second mother to Bessie and Kay. There is no grandchild. Bessie is marrying Ella's widower. Kay is the last of my daughters."

"Of course," I said. "It must have been a terrible time for your family. No wonder Kay doesn't talk about it."

Before another word could be spoken, Kay returned with Bessie. Mrs. Heunisch gave me a look, a signal to silence. Was the subject too raw to discuss before Kay and Bessie? It wasn't unusual for a sister to marry the widower of a sibling—a bit old-country—but not unheard of.

I extended my hand and said, "Congratulations, Bessie. I heard you are getting married."

Bessie responded with a smile and a nod. Kay said, "Oh, I *do* envy you, Bessie. Finally, a husband. You are everything a mother wants in a daughter, as she is quick to point out."

Was there a hint in Kay's remark? I couldn't tell. Maybe.

"George, why don't you stay for dinner?" Mrs. Heunisch asked, breaking the tension. "Now that Clarence and Mary have moved to their new home, we have two empty seats at the table. Please do join us."

"I'd be delighted. Home-cooked meals are hard to come by in Hawaii."

While Bessie and Mrs. Heunisch cooked, I helped Kay set the table, brushing against her as often as I dared. I managed a hug when we went into the butler's pantry for dishware. After Kay showed me which to choose, she left flustered, and I passed the dishes to her through the slide-up panel. I tugged at her hand when she reached for one, doing my best to sneak a kiss.

Kay said, "Later! Mother and Bessie are right there!"

The meal was as delicious as Kay and I dared to imagine home cooked meals with her. I loved her spark and couldn't wait for a moment alone with her. Playing footsie under the dinner table left a lot to be desired. I only had a month's vacation, and ten of those days were taken for the passage to and from Hawaii. Before I left for the evening, I asked, "May I take Kay to see Clarence's new home?"

"Yes, as long as Bessie is with you," Kay's mother replied.

After eating Ma's hearty breakfast the next day, I hopped the trolley car to Alameda.

Kay greeted me with, "Bessie is joining us as a chaperone for part of the way. She'll get off at Grand Avenue to shop while we continue to the Berkeley hills." The three of us walked arm-in-arm to catch the street car a few blocks from their house. I twisted in the seat to wave to Bessie when she was on the sidewalk at Grand, using it as an excuse to press my leg against Kay's.

We had to transfer once to get to Clarence's house, a two-story colonial beauty. Roses lined the walkway to the front porch, crowding the sidewalk. Kay snagged her skirt.

"Don't make a fuss." I cautioned. "If you say something negative about Mary's roses, she'll get upset."

We stayed for lunch after touring the house and garden. When Kay went to powder her nose, Clarence asked, "Did you hear the family story?"

"Yes," I replied. "I know all about Ella and Bessie. I don't see any problem with Bessie marrying Ella's widower."

"No, that's not it. There is a scandal surrounding Kay's grandfather. Ask Ma about it."

"What does that have to do with Kay? It would not be her fault if something bad happened. Geez, Clarence, no family is perfect. Look at ours. We're so driven that we don't care who we step on."

"Well, just find out. You are so taken by Kay you can't see straight."

My vacation days whipped by and I didn't give a damn about family secrets. Bessie chaperoned us as we made our way around the bay, and I was allowed one last night on the town alone with Kay because of my good behavior. I took her to the Palace Hotel for dinner again and gave her sapphire earrings to match the necklace I'd given her. She devoured me with kisses as my reward.

The following day Kay was at the mole to see me off. The morning mist clung to the water, and I threw a rose to her from the ferry, leaning a bit too far over the railing. The boat swayed and I teetered. Kay's hand flew to her mouth. She'd seen the rose and threw me a kiss when I righted myself. It was going to be a long six months.

chapter 6

The Ghost in the Closet

1920
Honolulu, Territory of Hawaii

When I returned to Honolulu, I slipped back into my daily routine. One of my jobs was controlling and directing radio transmissions for ships in the mid and South Pacific. The operators were like a pestilence. The station in Samoa annoyed us, Tahiti and Apia browbeat us, Alaska came weirdly through the static with their worries, and Frisco's demands were constant. Hawaii, Molokai, and Maui never gave us a moment's rest.[25]

Meanwhile Clarence persisted in digging up the scoop on the Heunisch family. Between him and Ma, they found out Adam Heunisch, Kay's grandfather, had committed suicide. Both pressed me to find out more.

I hadn't said a word to Kay about their discovery. She'd had a hard enough time talking about Ella's death. I certainly didn't want to upset her by asking pointed questions about her grandfather.

Kay wrote that Bessie had gotten married and left for Seattle. She said she was lonesome without her and couldn't wait for my return. I wrote saying nothing about her grandfather, but plenty about how much I missed her.

On my next trip home, I rushed into Kay's waiting arms. I'd gotten a raise to $190.00 per month plus a ten percent bonus. RCA was pleased with the increased traffic I'd generated and rewarded me accordingly.[26] I'd written to Clarence that I planned to ask Kay to marry me.

"Not before you find out about her family," he'd written back, forever playing the role of big-brother.

Because I declared my love, Clarence concluded that the Street clan should meet Kay and her mother. My brother Henry and his wife Norma, hosted a family dinner. Norma cooked for days, preparing a feast. The table stretched from one end of the dining room to the other, and white linen napkins embroidered with an "S" for Street graced each china plate. Candlelight sparkled from the silver and crystal. Kay was radiant in blue, wearing the sapphires I'd given her.

During dinner, Mrs. Heunisch asked, "George, how did you get into radio?"

"I caught the bug when I was about thirteen, in 1911. My neighbor taught me about radio and helped me build my first receiver. My detector was simple. I got a sewing needle from Ma and balanced it between two bits of carbon that I'd scavenged from gas streetlights when they were replaced."[27]

Ma joined in, "George set up a work table in the basement, and there was stuff everywhere. Capturing sounds from the ether. I couldn't believe it. You chewed the rag for hours on your set. I'd have to send one of your brothers to fetch you for bed."

"Ma, I loved it. We were pirates of the airwaves, listening to other's conversations, including the Navy's. The swear words I learned![28] Louis Clement, Staff Warner, F.D. Allen, and I spent hours 'talking' by Morse code. Remember when the neighbor got zapped because he touched the transmitter antenna that I'd strung along the top of the back fence?"[29]

"Oh, my gracious, yes. Our neighbor was fit to be tied."

"Where did you learn about all those dots and dashes?" Kay asked.

"In 1914, I passed a Department of Commerce examination for a Station License and Operators' License for my home location—6AB. So I dropped out of Poly-Hi for a term and took a course of study at Marconi wireless school in San Francisco in the Merchant's Exchange Building to upgrade to a commercial license. We had to sit hours on hard wooden seats, razor-straight shoulder-to-shoulder, pounding away either on our bugs or transcribing what we received through our earphones."[30]

"Bugs?" Kay asked.

"Yes, I made my first bug out of wood, razor blades, and baling wire.[31] A bug is the key used to tap out Morse code. We tap out the letters."

"How tedious," Kay said, "I could never do that."

"It's a man's job, Kay. There were no women in my class. Bob Carlisle, my instructor, helped me become a 'Coni Man.' My designation at Marconi was 'SE.'"

"SE, does that stand for Streetie?" Kay teased.

"Goodness, no." I retorted, hoping I'd never hear Streetie again.

"So you returned to high school after going to the wireless school? Mrs. Heunisch asked, coming to my rescue.

"Yes, I started a Radio Club but dropped out of school after receiving my commercial license. I didn't see the sense of sitting around drawing pictures when I could be working in wireless.[32] Pa was in complete agreement after the sinking of the *Titanic*."

Conversations tumbled around the table like a ship at sea. Things went swimmingly until my brother Ed—who had had one too many glasses of wine—said for all to hear, "So, Mrs. Heunisch, I understand your father-in-law committed suicide."

I dropped my fork. Mrs. Heunisch's hand flew to her chest.

"Ed, where did you hear such a thing?" I said, hoping to put an end to his rudeness.

"Why Clarence told me. You know we don't keep family secrets in this household. Ma remembers reading about a scandal years ago."

Henry interjected, "Ed, this is not the time!

Clarence piped up, "I only mentioned it to Ed because I thought he might remember something."

"It was years ago," Mrs. Heunisch said, "Kay was ten at the time."

Henry said, "Mrs. Heunisch, I apologize for my brother's rude behavior. Ed, let's drop the subject and continue our pleasant evening with these lovely ladies."

Then my sister Reta jumped in. "I want to hear what happened. If it was in the papers, surely it can be discussed."

I stood and said, "Please do not embarrass our guests!"

"George, it's okay," Mrs. Heunisch said. "Sit down. I have nothing to be ashamed of. Let me explain. There is no need to get upset."

I fumed at Clarence, Ed, and Reta. If they ruined my chances with Kay, I'd never forgive them.

"Mrs. Heunisch, please do not feel obligated," I said. "My opinion of you and your family will not change no matter what you say. I hold you in the highest regard."

Mrs. Heunisch eyes filled with gratitude.

"I remember now," Ma interjected, "I remember reading something. Wasn't there an article about a park and lost money?

Kay interrupted with a catch in her voice, "I miss Grandfather," she said. "I remember the fundraiser—the graphophones and kinetoscopes and magic lanterns. I loved peeking into the kinetoscope and watching the moving pictures."

"Yes," Mrs. Heunisch replied. "The fundraiser for the park was in the papers. Perhaps it is the one Mother Street read about."

"There was something else," Ma said. "I can't put my finger on it."

Mrs. Heunisch sighed and continued. "You may have read about my father-in-law, Adam Heunisch. He owned Abrahamson-Heunisch Glass Company which merged with Illinois-Pacific Glass. When he retired, he had every intention of turning it over to his son — my husband, Albert Gustave.

"Oh, that's where Kay got her middle name "Alberta?" I said, hoping to break the tension. "Kathryn Alberta."

"Yes, Albert and I didn't have a son, so we passed on his name to Kathryn. Anyway, Adam was a millionaire, a member of San Francisco's high society. They lived in a three-story Queen Ann on Baker Street. It was perfect for entertaining."

"That's why Kay loves parties," I said to steer the conversation in a more gentile direction.

"Perhaps. Her grandparents' threw many a party for the girls. Adam took Kay everywhere, showing her off and delighting her with the wonders of the world. She was the apple of his eye. They were constant companions and he spoiled her horribly."

"Well, that explains why Kay loves the finer things in life," I said. "It sounds like she had a fairy tale upbringing, which was well deserved."

Then Ed blurted, "If he was so well off and well-liked, why did he commit suicide?"

"Ed I said. "Stop being crass."

"It's okay," Mrs. Heunisch said, "Adam was a dreamer. He only wanted the best for his granddaughters, so he came up with the idea of creating the greatest amusement park in the United States. He called it Dreamland and hosted a fundraiser—the one Kay remembers. It was the talk of the town. Adam spared no expense. Chartered ferries and cars transported guests to a lavishly decorated wooded glen in Marin Country, where the park would be. Fairies, magicians, ponies, and musicians mingled among the guests. Investors opened their wallets, and construction began." [33]

"Oh yes, my husband's family was invited," Reta said. "Didn't Dreamland go over budget?"

"Yes, that's right," Mrs. Heunisch said.

I said, "I'd love to see it."

Mrs. Heunisch said, "There's nothing left. Not a trace."

Ed said, "You are that Heunisch? I thought Dreamland was a crazy idea from the start. Who would take their children to see life-size castles and pirate ships? Kids are supposed to grow up, not get lost in a fantasy world like George did when he listened to the voices coming through the ether. It spoils them!"

I said, "You sound like Dad and his 'children should be seen and not heard' mandates. How will children become inventive if they don't have imaginations?"

"Poppycock!" Retorted Ed, and he took another sip of wine.

Reta added, "Well, at least he bought real estate. Did he manage to hang on to that?"

Henry said, "Reta, that's a very personal question and none of our business."

"I don't mind," Mrs. Heunisch said, "It's better to have everything out in the open. It was all over the papers anyway. Adam raided the family coffers to cover shortfalls and mortgaged our house and the land. Dreamland became a nightmare. He tried to regain his investors' money by speculating in the stock market. When things went from bad to worse, he lost everything and started drinking. His doctor sent him to the St. Helena Sanitarium, but he never recovered. He committed suicide in 1908 by drinking carbolic acid."

An image of a foaming mouth filled my brain. If Mrs. Heunisch wanted to end the conversation by shocking us, she succeeded.

Surprise swept across our faces. Kay remained silent. I could tell it was hard for her to hear the naked truth and witness the looks on the faces of my family.

"How horrible for the family," I said, recovering. "What did you do?"

"We moved to Oakland. My husband went to Seattle to run the Illinois-Pacific operation there."

Reta asked, "Why didn't you go to Seattle with him?"

"Good grief, Reta, it's none of our business!"

Before I could say another word, Mrs. Heunisch said, "He fell in love with someone else, and I divorced him. That is why I run a boarding house." And she glared at Reta, daring her to press her further.

Before sparks flew, I said, "Well, my pa taught me there is no shame in failure. 'That is how one learns,' he used to say. I will certainly not think less of you or Kay because of his tragedy." I took Kay's hand. Her family story clarified a lot—her vanity, secretiveness, and free spirit.

Reta, always the one to have the last word, said, "Well, at least now all the ghosts are out of the closet." She left the table, dropping her napkin on the chair.

I offered my best assurances, "Mrs. Heunisch, thank you for sharing your story. You bravely faced my brothers and haughty sister. I promise you that your situation doesn't affect my feelings for Kay or you. On the contrary, I find Kay more endearing. Norma, Henry, thank you for the delicious dinner. I think it's time I drove these two ladies home. They probably have had enough of the Street family for one night."

Before we left, I cornered my siblings in the parlor. "Your behavior tonight was inexcusable. How dare you put the woman I love in such an embarrassing position?"

Ed said, "Don't marry her, Streeeetie. She's spoiled. I bet she's never worked a day in her life."

"She's a looker, for sure," Clarence said. "But there's not much between her ears."

Reta added, "I agree. She's flighty, self-centered, and soft. You'll regret having her around."

"You three have always tried to run my life! How can you know what she's like? You didn't give her a chance, and you crucified her mother in front of her. Henry doesn't object to my marrying her. You can go to hell." I left them gaping and walked to the hall to help Kay and Mrs. Heunisch with their coats.

"I'm so sorry about my siblings' rude behavior," I told Mrs. Heunisch as she shrugged into her coat. "Kay, please don't hold their unpleasantness against me. They have always been overbearing." We drove in silence, and when I walked them to the door, Kay only offered her hand in farewell.

When I returned home, I told Ma, "I can't believe Clarence, Ed, and Reta. How dare them! Kay's family's fall from grace makes no difference to me. I plan to propose to Kay before I leave for Hawaii. They certainly won't be invited to our wedding."

"Now, George, don't be such a hot head. They are only looking out for you as they always have," Ma said.

"Yeah, like the time Ed boxed my ears, or Clarence helped himself to my stuff? Reta was forever telling on me. No thanks, Ma, I'm done with them."

Ma shook her head and said, "Well, I hope it works out for you. Kay comes from a different world. She will expect a lot from you."

"I hope she does. I will make her the toast of Hawaii," and I left the room more determined than ever to prove my family wrong.

I bought Kay a ring with sapphires and diamonds to match the necklace I'd given her. On my last night, I borrowed Henry's car and took her for a night on the town. During dinner at the Palace Hotel, I slipped the ring into her Coca-Cola when I spiked it with rum. She took a couple of sips before she spotted it. That's when I popped the question. "Will you marry me?" I asked, and I dropped to one knee.

She fished it out, radiating, and slipped it on her finger after licking off the cola. "Yes," she said, "yes, yes, darling." The diners at the next table applauded. I leaned across the table and kissed her. Kay tugged my ear with her teeth and whispered, "You are my knight in shining armor." And I kissed her again.

chapter 7

Paradise Lost

1921-1923
Honolulu, Territory of Hawaii

By July of 1921, I'd saved enough money to rent a furnished house on Cleghorn Drive, four blocks from Waikiki Beach. Kay and I picked a date, and I booked passage for Kay and her mother on *SS Wilhelmina*. It wasn't a luxury liner, but it wasn't a tramp steamer either. I got a kick out of the fact that *Wilhelmina* was her grandmother's given name and hoped the connection would demonstrate my sensitivity to their family history.

Kay had never been on a passenger liner, so she was understandably nervous. Earthquakes rattled her, but vast expanses of water with no land in sight terrified her. She did not know how to swim. I had flowers delivered to their room, hoping it would ease her mind.

The five-day crossing was an agony for me. Kay finally arrived on the twelfth of July, and I greeted them with plumeria leis. Kay lifted the flowers to her nose, inhaled, and then clasped me in her arms, pleased to have her feet on land again. She and her mother stayed with my sister, Anna, and her new husband, Leo G. Fehlman, Advertising Manager for the Honolulu Star-Bulletin.

Within a week of Kay's arrival, we married. Anna and Leo were our witnesses. A handful of guests attended our wedding at the Central Union Church, a typical New England-style building with a spire and Greek columns. It seemed out of place among the rattling palm trees, but it was majestic enough for Kay. She was beautiful. I was restless. We left the reception early.

I booked an ocean-view suite at the Moana Hotel in the new Italian Renaissance wing for our wedding night. Kay draped herself on our bed wearing only a boa, and I devoured her with passion. I don't think she was prepared for the consequences of her teasing. She was a tense lover and crept out of bed, so that I wouldn't ravish her again.

Her mother returned to the mainland within days. She handed Kay a book in parting. *Vivilore* was about life and proper living, complete with anatomical drawings, passed on from her grandmother.

She read page 276 to me: "When love gives place to lust, it must die, for as Prof. Fowler shows, the two are directly opposed to each other." It suggested that "Continuing in ignorant excesses, the moral, intelligent and physical powers become impaired; puny, sickly children are born...." And it stated that the "female admits the male in a sexual embrace only for procreation." [34]

I took the book and read the entire chapter titled, "The Sexual Embrace" to get a feel for what I was up against. It talked about perfect obedience, purity of love, abstinence, avoiding stimulating food and drinks, and thinking beautiful thoughts. I liked the part about perfect obedience, but that hardly suited Kay.

Aerial of Kahuku *(Courtesy of California Historical Radio Society*

We honeymooned on the island, and I introduced her to the tropical paradise she would now call home. I took her to Koko Head, the Blow Hole, and drove her to the Kahuku station on the north end. We picnicked on the beach, and marveled at the turtles floating in the turquoise surf.

After we settled into our new home, Kay asked, "What am I supposed to do all day while you are at work?"

"Well, you can keep the place clean, fix me a nice dinner, and do what wives everywhere do," I replied.

"I don't know how to cook anything but fried chicken. Mother and Bessie did all the cooking and cleaning at the boarding house.

Before, we had a maid. Can't we hire a maid and a cook? Can't we go out?" she cooed.

"No, we can't. I'm not made of money. We're comfortable but not rich. You need to help out."

"You said I could have anything I wanted. You said you'd pamper me like a princess," she whined.

"Within reason, Kay. I'm sure you can keep house and cook. Every woman does. I'll fix cocktails while you fix dinner." She banged pots in the kitchen and crafted a meal that left a lot to be desired.

I took her out dancing when I could, but not as often as she wanted. I admit I did enjoy showing her off. She turned heads. However, I was surprised that marriage hadn't dampened her flirtations with other men.

"Kay, we are mentioned in the RCA *World Wide Wireless* newsletter," I said one afternoon in September after a long, muddy drive from Kokohead.

"What does it say? Read it to me."

It says, "Street, by the way, is a newlywed. Many a crepe is seen these days. Fair mourners have lost their George, but George has a wonderful little wife and though we all hated to see him leave the bachelor quarters here, we know that he has gone one better up on the road to life. Much happiness and best wishes to you, George."[35]

"Wonderful little wife? Is that all they said about me? Who are all these mourners they are talking about? Didn't you behave while I was waiting for you?"

"I had girlfriends before I met you, just like you had suitors. You are the one I married," and I gave her a reassuring hug. "Now be a wonderful little wife and fix me dinner. I'm starved."

Kay spent her days walking, window shopping, and sunning at the beach when the heat stifled and muffled sounds and the beaky-looking Bird of Paradise flowers drooped. Her bathing suit exposed way too much flesh, in my opinion. She loved to have other men fawn over her and used marriage like a stop sign when things got heated. Whenever I said anything, she would sweep her arm upward, cock her hip and say, "Oh George, don't be silly. I only have eyes for you."

Then she embarrassed me at the Christmas party. The party was at the Koko Head resident hall, and it lasted all day. We played tennis in the morning and swam at the beach in the afternoon. Even the sea couldn't shush the sound of her as she giggled with delight at the words and whistles that passing admirers lobbed her way. I took her on a short hike to Sacred Falls for a picnic with other "city folk" looking for an outing. She held court, reclining at the base of the waterfall like a Greek goddess. Then she asked an associate, "Would you for a big red apple?"

"Kay, that was humiliating! You can't talk like that to my business associates," I told her as soon as we got in the car to head back to our house. A hurricane, locally called a Kona storm, was brewing, and I wanted to beat it home before the rain and wind overwhelmed the island.

"Why not?" She retorted, her blue eyes flashing. "He had his hands all over me. Why can he flirt, and I can't?"

"You can't because you are my *wife*. You must behave like a married woman now. You make me look like a fool, like a man who doesn't have control over his life. You must stop. It could mean my job." That's when our honeymoon ended, and the fights began.

As I drove, lightning cracked the sky, and the rain hissed like bacon in a frypan. I sat in silence while "Kona" Kay fumed.

The Kona storm smashed ashore just before Christmas. It tore the ocean apart. Walls of waves stirred to new heights. Winds took out power and telegraph lines and buckled the palms. Leaves scuttled like crabs along the streets, bringing the heady smell of the sea to our front door. Fortunately, the alternator equipment at Kahuku held, and wireless traffic from the mainland was not disrupted. However, the underwater cable at Midway broke, forcing Japanese traffic onto our circuits.[36] We handled the increase, but I saw little of Kay during that time.

She was not happy. Like a petulant child, she'd pout, storm out of the room, fling herself onto the couch, and give me the silent treatment. And when that didn't work, she blustered like a hurricane. When I indulged her, she opened herself to me. When I didn't, it was "Katy bar the door." The damage rendered during our imagined passion collided like freight trains, and the wreckage spilled all over the tracks. I wondered if she'd ever settle down. And then she got pregnant. I was delighted—and hopeful. Surely, motherhood would cool her heels.

In July, we attended a farewell party at Kahuku. John Finch's two-year stint was over, and he was headed back to the mainland.[37] Kay flirted about even though she was five months pregnant. The next day Finch hosted a luncheon, and Kay could not behave. After that, I stopped taking her to business functions. She'd get all dolled up and yell when I walked out the door without her.

In November of 1922, she gave me a son, George Junior. I was delighted and hoped she'd straighten out now that she had a baby. I had pampered her during her pregnancy, helped her with the baby's room, cooked, and did my best to make her comfortable. I also rented a larger home on Tusitala, a block from Cleghorn. The street was named after Robert Louis Stevenson, who took the Samoan name of

George and George Jr. in front of banyan tree *(George Street Archive)*

Tusitala, which means "Teller of Tales." Stevenson penned a poem under a banyan tree to Princess Kaiulani that I suspected was located to the right of our house. Kay would lounge under the tree and ask me to recite poetry to her as though she were Princess Kaiulani. I obliged. Anything to keep her happy for my child's sake.

When George Jr. arrived, she expected me to continue to indulge her even after a long workday. By then, Koko Head's administrative operations had been transferred to the second story of 923 Fort Street. When the landline to Koko Head was dismantled, I worked out of the Honolulu office. The signals from Koko Head were converted to an audio frequency and amplified for recording and telephone circuits. We'd monitor the signals, which had different tones for different stations. A similar arrangement was made with the

San Francisco office, and by September 25th, RCA had wireless communication between Honolulu and San Francisco.[38]

Our new house was closer to the office so I didn't have to battle the roads on a daily basis. The Fort Street center had a large eight-paneled bowed window with stained glass transoms that filled the space with prisms of light. However, the wooden frame around them was honey-combed by an ant infestation reminding me of lace.

One night an army of flying ants swarmed the office seeking the light. The operator on duty covered himself and his machine in mosquito netting and kept working. By late morning—and six dust pans full of wings later—the office was back to normal.

Occasionally, Kay would often join me for lunch as we attempted to keep our marriage on track. We settled into a routine for George Jr.'s sake, but my dreams of a perfect family life turned into a muddled river of tumbling reveries when I caught her flirting at the beach with George Jr. in tow.

Exasperated, I said I lost it. "Kay, you need to be a housewife and a mother, not a flirt on the beach with a baby in tow. I expected you to fulfill your role as wife and mother dutifully, just as your mother and my mother have done."

Kay spit back, clearly offended, "You said I could have whatever my heart desired. You said I would be the princess of the island. All I am is a housemaid and diaper changer. I want a nanny."

"We can't afford one. Start acting like a wife!" I responded, and, of course, tears flowed, and the baby cried.

I tried. I spent time with George Jr. on my days off and took him to the beach with my friends to give Kay a break. It was never enough. Kay always wanted more and openly flirted with any adult male who stopped by, which infuriated me.

I found it impossible to have an intellectual conversation with her. She focused on gossip magazines, fortune tellers, and the latest rags about the rich and famous. Our lovemaking became wooden. My sister Anna could not stand her and had no interest in spending time with my self-centered wife.

In the fall of 1923, RCA offered me a promotion to the radio marine division in Seattle. As much as I hated to leave Hawaii, I jumped at the deal. Paradise without happiness was just a jungle. Kay and I were like caged tigers, always snarling and clawing at each other. When we spat our thoughts, there remained a lingering static in the air electrified by anger. There was no need to decode the meaning of our words. They came through crystal clear with no interference. And they hurt.

I held out hope that by going stateside, Kay would connect with her family and become a good wife. Her sister Bessie lived in Seattle and had children. Surely, she could take Kay under her wing and teach her how to be a proper mother. George Jr.—Georgie—had captured my heart, and I was determined to give him the best upbringing possible, even if it meant moving.

"Kay, we're going to Seattle," I announced the moment I walked in the door. Georgie was crying, trapped in his playpen. I grabbed him and swung him in the air. "Georgie, you're going to meet your grandmas. Kay, did you hear what I said?"

Kay was making cocktails, looking smug. She wore a new dress and had her boa around her neck.

"How do you like me in my new dress?" she asked flipping her boa, not reacting to my proclamation. She had painted pink toenails to match the flowers in the dress she hadn't asked if she could buy.

"You know you need to ask before you buy something. Why did you buy a new dress?"

"I'm princess, queen of the world," she said as she fluttered about the room. "I wanted it."

"You wanted it? Don't you think you should have asked?" I steamed, struggling to control my temper and ignore her impertinence. "RCA has offered me the district manager position of the Pacific Northwest, and I accepted. We will be moving to Seattle in October. You may not buy any more new dresses. Keep that one, if you must, but do not buy anything more without my approval. We have to save for the move. We'll spend time in Oakland first so Georgie can meet our families." She handed me a drink and took a gulp of her own while she processed the news.

"Apparently, I have no say in the matter. Why do I always have to do what you say?"

"Because I am the husband and make the money."

"It will be nice to be near Bessie."

"That's what I thought."

"Will your promotion mean more money?" she asked. "Can we book first class? Where will we stay in Oakland? I don't want to be with your family. They were terrible the last time we were with them."

"Yes, of course, I'll get a raise. I'll increase your household budget and spending money accordingly. RCA will pay for our transfer and passage. First class but not a suite."

"Well, that's something. Can we have a going away party?"

"Yes," I agreed, knowing a party would cheer her up. "Keep the cost down. Invite who you want and do it soon. I'll send a radiogram to our mothers to let them know we are coming to visit before relocating to Seattle."

"Oh, George, the party will be so much fun. I'll wear my new dress. Can I have it catered? We'll go out with a bang, *darling*." She said, mimicking Tallulah Bankhead. She swept through the house, all smiles, flipping her boa, lifting her skirt to show her garter drink, in hand. That night she made love enthusiastically. Perhaps the move to Seattle was just the ticket for better days ahead.

chapter 8

Wits' End

1923-1927
Seattle, Washington

On 2 October 1923, Kay and I boarded *SS Maui* for San Francisco, a combined passenger and cargo liner. The ship was a bit worn in places but sound. White table-clothed settings formalized its low-ceilinged dining hall, although Kay voiced her disappointment about the ship's lack of luxury. Kay was excited about returning home, and for five days I enjoyed myself for the most part. Unbeknownst to us, Kay was one month pregnant. Waves of nausea overtook her, which we attributed to sea sickness not morning sickness.

The following month at her mother's boarding house where we stayed, she said, "George, I'm pregnant," and my world stopped.

"Kay, are you sure? That's wonderful!" I said, delighted, worried, and fearful all at the same time. We made beautiful babies, but could we raise them? I wasn't so sure anymore.

"Of course, I'm sure. I went to the doctor, and he confirmed it. How could you do this to me? I was just getting my figure back after Georgie. Now I'm going to balloon like a blimp."

"Kay, we're having a baby. Georgie will have a brother or sister." I said, hoping to raise her spirits as I gathered her in my arms. "I'll take as much time off as possible." And I kissed her hair. "You are glowing already."

Kay pulled back and whimpered, "I can't have the baby in Seattle. I won't have it there. My sister died in Seattle having hers. After I went to the doctor, I visited a fortune teller. She warned me that something bad might happen."

"A fortune teller?" I said in disbelief. "You can't be serious. My job is in Seattle. We have to go. Maybe the fortune teller meant something bad would happen if we didn't go."

"I'm sure she was referring to the baby. I will not have it in Seattle. I don't care if I'm superstitious. I'm tired. Little Georgie is a handful. I am going to stay here so Ma can help me."

"I can't be in two places at once. I can't afford to lose my job with RCA. I have to go."

"She flopped on the bed and put her hand on her forehead as though fainting. "How can you leave me? How can you leave us? You don't love me. You don't love Georgie."

We'd been through this before. Georgie's birth had been a terror of pain and fear for Kay. Her mother came for the birth, but neither of us could comfort her during her labor. Kay was convinced she would die even though she had no complications and was in the best maternity facility in Honolulu. I tried to understand her current anguish, but it wasn't easy.

"You know that's not true."

As usual, she created the problem and expected me to fix it. Her mother had rented our room in anticipation of our move. Ma was still grieving Pa's death and had little patience with Kay. I had to figure something out quickly.

"How about if you stay here for the birth, then join me? That way, you'll have two mothers to help. I'll return when you are close to your due date."

"Leave me here. Leave your son. I don't want to die."

I didn't know what to say. So much drama, so much selfishness. Today, I did find it hard to love her. Georgie, however, was my shining star. He would be the one I'd find hard to leave.

Because her mother had rented our rooms, I bought a house at 1321 Bates Rd, near her mother's in the Trestle Glen District of Oakland. My sister Reta was doing quite well in real estate, and encouraged me to buy. At the very least, I was making a good investment.

Kay loved the house and the location. It was a three-bedroom English Tudor. The streetcar that connected the neighborhood to the Lakeshore Avenue shopping district was right around the corner. I moved them in before I left for Seattle.

Kay gave birth to Barbara Jean on the third of June, 1924, shortly after I returned to be with her. A boy and a girl. Barbara Jean was the female version of me, dark-eyed and dark-haired. Georgie took after Kay, blond and blue-eyed. Our family was complete; now, if only I could hold it together.

Before I returned to Seattle, we catered a cocktail party to introduce Barbara to the family. Kay was not ready to travel, and I planned to return in a couple of months to help her on the train.

When the party was well underway—I made sure there was plenty of booze—Ed took me aside, "George, you've got a beautiful girl and boy. Who's going to take care of your kids when you move your family to Seattle? Kay lets Ma do all the fussing over them. I haven't seen her hold Barbara since I've been here. Can Kay even change a diaper?"

"Why do you care? It's none of your business how we raise our children. Kay loves them. It's just that she enjoys being fussed over too. Tell her how great she looks. That'll make her happy. She worries about her figure constantly."

Most of my siblings attended. We caught up while they passed around my children like baggage. Clarence made a point of complementing Kay. Reta, not so much.

The next day, I headed for Seattle and rented a three-bedroom apartment for us in the heart of the city. It was within walking distance of streetcars and a park. By late December, I moved my little family after Ma bought the Bates property from me. Ma wanted a new house since Pa was no longer around, and I needed the cash.

Kay, George Jr., and Barbara in the stroller
c. 1924 *(George Street Archive)*

Every day that didn't rain, Kay took Barbara out in the stroller with Georgie holding on to the side. But having a second child did not bring us closer together. Kay was at her wit's end trying to run a household and care for an infant and toddler without the help of our mothers. Her sister, Bessie, wasn't much help; she had her own life to lead. I hired a maid to clean once a week. If I hadn't, I'd never hear the end of it.

To make matters worse, I couldn't help Kay with the children because my work required a lot of travel. I was in charge of installing and maintaining wireless radio equipment for commercial shipping and fishing fleets in the Pacific Northwest and Alaska. As a consequence, Kay and I were at each other's throats when I was home. Little Georgie would hide, and Barbara would cry. And I was at a loss.

"This is not the life you promised," Kay reminded me. "How can you be so mean? I need a Nanny. Your children need a Nanny. Bessie has a Nanny."

Lt. George Street, USNR
Commander of Volunteer
Communication Reserve,
pictured left.
(George Street Archive)

"Kay, I can't afford one. Bessie married a bacteriologist, a man of science. They live in their family's home. We have to pay rent. I'm doing the best I can. I've even joined the Naval Reserves to bring in more money. What more do you want me to do? Try being a good wife and mother. Clean the house yourself. That would save us money."

"I can't do it all. I'm not supposed to do it all. Why did I ever marry you? You don't take care of me. All you do is fuss over the children. How about me? Fix me a toddy. I can't do this anymore," and she struck her usual pose, with her unlit cigarette holder pointed at the ceiling.

Our disagreements turned into tornadoes, swirling with discontent that destroyed everything in their wake. Kay wanted things I could not afford, and I wanted her to be like my mother. Her relentless need for attention drove me up the wall. She continued to flirt at company and now Navy functions, so I stopped taking her once again. I would not have her risqué behavior jeopardize my position. "Oh, George," she'd say when I confronted her, "I was just having a bit of fun." She didn't seem to understand how much she embarrassed me.

To escape, I threw myself into work and traveled every chance I got. I installed radiotelegraph stations in canneries along the coast of Oregon, Washington, and Alaska.

In August 1925, I and three others took two portable Radiolas super heterodynes, models 24 and 26, into the Black Diamond Coal Mine, seventeen miles southeast of Seattle.

George Street on the left at the Black Diamond Mine
(George Street Archive)

Alaska and southern California could pick up KTCL but not stations east of the Cascade foothills. We wanted to try to pick up Seattle radio station KTCL, located in the Home Saving Building, at different depths to see if the coal beds absorbed or deflected radio waves.

At the mine entrance, we pulled on coveralls and donned helmets with lamps. KTCL came in loud and clear at the surface. We traversed horizontally two thousand feet, forty-five feet above sea level. There we picked up only a whisper. We couldn't obtain any signal after descending to the lower levels, either with a loop or a ground antenna, so we concluded that the coal beds did absorb the radio waves.[39]

On a whim, I supervised the installation of the first shipboard remote control center for tuning in radio broadcasting programs. On the Ketchikan run, the passengers aboard *SS Northland* could listen to music. I had gone around town and bought sets and parts for around five hundred dollars. When the news hit the papers, Japan wanted a similar set-up on their Seattle-Orient passenger ships. However, RCA took a dim view of what I had done because they planned on doing similar installations for several thousand dollars instead of five hundred dollars.[40]

Then the radiotelegraphy and theory instructor at the local YMCA asked me to step in and teach while he took a six-week leave. I agreed in exchange for a class on public speaking. So just about every evening for weeks, I was either teaching or taking a course at the Seattle YMCA, which did not sit well with Kay.

"You're never home. Georgie and Barbara hardly know you," she'd rant, laying on the guilt. There was nothing I could say to ease the tension.

Barbara Jean and George Jr. C. 1926 *(George Street Archive)*

Soon I was on the speech circuit, giving interviews and educating interested parties about wireless' new technology, which included sending photographs over the airwaves and synchronizing motion pictures with voices. General J. G. Harbord, President of RCA, predicted that the Jazz Age would end with the new broadcasting capabilities of radio. I hoped it would work for our marriage's sake. Kay was hooked on Jazz and wanted to go dancing almost every night. Her interest in my work only surfaced when I made the newspapers.

Before seven hundred people at a Chamber of Commerce luncheon, I presented a radio telephotograph, an electronic facsimile (fax) of an RCA radiogram sent from the Honolulu Chamber of

Commerce. It was probably the first telephotograph ever projected on a screen before an audience.[41] It was transmitted from Honolulu to San Francisco and then flown to Seattle by special arrangement. Since it was my first address in front of a large audience, I spent hours preparing and practicing my twenty-minute speech. Then, the Chamber invited an out-of-towner to speak at the last minute, and I had to cut my prepared remarks by five minutes. My knees literally shook when I was called upon but I managed to get on my feet.[42]

After my speech, word got out about radio telephotography transmissions, and the next thing I knew, management at Meier & Frank department store in Portland, Oregon, wanted to see me. The Big Boss scared the wits out of me. He said, "Well, young man, what is this thing about pictures by wireless?" His abruptness is what got to me.

I explained telephotography, and he responded, "Okay, we will use it. I want the latest Paris designs in a half-page ad as soon as possible."

He turned to the fellow who brought me in and said, "Go ahead and make arrangements with our Paris, France office."[43]

The Morning Oregonian, 16 August 1926. *(George Street Archive)*

On 16 August 1926, The *Morning Oregonian* newspaper in Portland featured—on the front page—drawings of dresses by Paris fashion designers sent by radio telephotography. "Sketched by our Paris office artists Friday morning, rushed to London by airplane, transmitted by telephotograph to New York, then by telephotograph to San Francisco, finally by airplane to Portland," the subtitle read.[44]

My boss in New York was pleased, and Kay was pleased. She liked seeing my name in the papers, and she'd gotten a new dress out of the deal from Meier & Frank. Following this publicity, I was in more demand and gave talks in Washington and Vancouver, B.C. I also had the honor of installing the first direction finder on a ship in the Pacific area for RCA, hailed as the most significant aid to navigation since ships began sailing the seas.

Then in 1927, radio changed. Congress passed a bill that specified that the government owned the airwaves, and it formed the Federal Radio Commission (FRC)[2] to license operating frequencies for broadcasting.[45] Previously, parties using the same frequency created a free-for-all of garbled and tangled messages. Once the FRC assigned frequency bands, some of RCA's existing radio equipment became obsolete in the Pacific Northwest, particularly in the Alaskan fisheries.

While in Washington D. C. at a Naval Reserve training session, I attended the Congressional hearings debating the upcoming changes. Working with RCA's Vice President, W.A. Winterbottom, I helped negotiate an extension of the deadline so RCA and G.E. could manufacture new equipment, which I helped plan and design.[46]

---

[2]Now, the Federal Communications Commission (FCC).

That didn't make the papers. All Kay acknowledged was a husband who was never home. Her pouting and complaints hit a fever pitch.

And then there was Stella Cayo, my secretary. She wore cloche hats like Kay, but she couldn't have been more different. During the Great War, she ran the Marconi office by herself, and now she commanded my office like a naval officer.[47] Experiencing such efficiency, dedication, and intelligence made me realize that the only good thing about my marriage was the children.

Kay wanted Jazz-age freedom and pampering over family and my career, just like Mrs. Winthrop in the movie Kay had seen years ago. She hadn't learned the lesson her mother had hoped for by watching the film. My mother was right when she said, "How could someone like her settle down and raise a family?" I should have listened to Ma. It galled me to no end to admit defeat. Ed and Reta would say, "I told you so."

In August 1927, I wrote:

```
Dear Ma,

...What I am going to tell you, Ma, I know you
will probably take it pretty hard, but I know,
too, you have seen quite a bit of my domestic
difficulties and feel you realize I sincerely
tried to make my home everything it should have
been. After so many years of what seemed a
futile effort on my part, receiving no help from
her, and after careful thought, I decided that
not only was I unhappy, but she would be more
and more so as time went on. Then, too, I could
not stand the thought of having the children
brought up under such unhappy and stressed
conditions. So, I did what I sincerely thought
```

was the only thing to do. Several days ago, the interlocutory decree of divorce was granted. Her mother came here about a month ago and was here during the time we agreed to end our marriage. I would have liked very much to have had custody of the children. It was possible that I could have had George but thought it best not to separate them if I could not have them both. I believe they are all in Oakland now and expect to establish their home there. Kay had many good qualities, and the whole thing was in our different mental make-ups, I guess.

Your loving son,
George[48]

chapter 9

East with the Radio

1930
Japan

In the fall of 1930, my head was on the chopping block at Seattle's Radiomarine division due to the Great Depression. They shut down the entire division with little notice. America was in a tailspin. Banks closed, fortunes were lost, and work disappeared. Stella Cayo returned to RCA's telegraph office, and I headed to Ma's to see my children and look for a new position.

My supervisor, T.M. Stevens, went to bat for me but then, on 11 November, sent a confidential memo …"I made efforts to get you a good lineup with RCA Photophone and with RCA Victor but, due to the general business depression, was unsuccessful in getting immediate favorable action. Both concerns have promised to do what they can as soon as conditions change for the better."[49] Not good news. My savings ran low, and I didn't want to miss Kay's support payments.

But luck was on my side. Within a couple of weeks, Stevens called, "George, I found a position for you."

"Thank goodness. Tell me about it."

"Don't get too excited," Stevens said, "It's a temporary position with RCA-Communications. Sarnoff has convinced the board that broadcasting is the way forward because they made sixty-five million compared to RCA's International Communication's four and a half million. He spun off communications to position it for a possible sale, perhaps to International Telephone and Telegraph (ITT)."[50]

Who will head the division? I asked.

"Art Isbell. He's a good man. He became the General Superintendent of the Pacific Division about the time Sarnoff became General Manager in June of 1921."

"I've heard of him. Maybe I met him once. How soon will the sale happen?"

"Nobody knows. We've had word that ITT wants to expand. We are going to increase our markets to make the sale sweeter. Right now, George Shecklen, who is in Shanghai, wants to take a vacation, and RCA needs someone to fill his shoes and boost business. You fit the bill because you've been to the Orient. I recommended you."

"Thank you! I know "Sheck." We are in the same unit in the Naval Reserves. When do I leave?"

"Does the week after Christmas work for you?" Stevens asked.

"That's perfect."

I put the receiver down relieved to know I'd have a paycheck again. I could indulge the children, buying them new clothes and taking them to the movies, the zoo, and the park. I would host a dinner party for George Jr.'s eighth birthday without trepidation. God, it's better to have money than not.

I stuck my head into the living room and said, "Ma, I'll be out of your hair soon." She was in her favorite chair, knitting in front of the fire. Her needles stopped clicking.

"You found work?" she asked.

"Yes! I'm headed for Japan and China again. It's a temporary position, but its work. I'll have a steady income and an expense account, and can live cheaply. I don't want to miss my support payments to Kay. Fifty dollars a month is a lot when no prospects are on the horizon."

"How long will you be gone?" she asked. "The kids are going to miss you. I don't think Kay gives them much attention. They seem happy with you around. George Jr. has become protective and more self-confident. Ever since they witnessed a car careen into the Colonnade by the lake, he looks out for her.[51] He takes Barbara's hand when they cross the street on the way to school."

"He's a good boy. I'll write him every chance I get. I'll be gone for less than a year, and I'll try to get something close to home when I return."

"Do you want me to keep your room open while you're gone?"

"I'd appreciate having a place to stay when I return. Will you look out for George and Barbara while I'm gone? Kay is so flighty; I worry about her squandering my support payments instead of caring for the children. As long as they live under the same roof as Kay's mother, I know they'll be okay. The kids adore Grandma Heunisch, Mabel. I think they like her better than Kay."

"Is Kay looking for work? Ma asked.

"As far as I know, she is. Two of the units in her mother's fourplex on Montecito are vacant. I guess Kay's trying to help her mother make ends meet. George Jr. told me she comes home with swollen feet after a day of pounding the pavement."

"Do you think she's using your support payments to help her mother?" Ma asked.

"I don't know. Kay says it's none of my business. She has a couple of new dresses, though. George Jr. says Kay makes them a big pot of macaroni and cheese with

Kay and Barbara c. 1930
(George Street Archive)

beans, and that's about all they eat. The kids take it to school in their lunch pail. Fortunately, they like it and don't seem to mind. They're both growing like weeds, so whatever she's feeding them seems to be doing the job."

"I'll keep an eye on them and reach out to Mabel. Have you told Kay that you'll be leaving?"

"Not yet, but I will. I hate leaving the children again, but this is a good opportunity for me and my career. I'd be a fool to turn it down. I don't have to go until after the holidays, so we'll have a jolly time at Thanksgiving and Christmas. Santa will bring lots of presents for them."

The following day I petitioned the Naval Reserve to grant me temporary leave from duty as Commander of the Volunteer Communication Reserve since I couldn't serve while overseas. I also wrote a letter to Mr. Stevens and Mr. Isbell, thanking them for their efforts on my behalf.[52]

Two days after Christmas, with a head full of fond memories and a heart heavy with the pain of parting, I sailed for Yokohama, Japan, aboard *SS President Jackson*. The crossing gave me time to reflect and worry since I wasn't crewing this time. I could only hope I'd made the right decision. I wrote to Ma about how this separation business was the bunk where the kiddies were concerned, especially when I wanted them so badly. Ma, always my guiding light, sent me a poem I now carry in my wallet:

> Build for yourself a strong box.
> Fashion each part with care;
> When it's strong as your hand can make it,
> Put all your troubles there.
> Hide there all thought of your failure,
> And each bitter cup that you quaff.
> Lock all your heartaches within it,
> And sit on the lid and laugh.
> Tell no one else of its contents;
> Never its secrets share;
> When you've dropped in your cares and worry,
> Drop them forever there.
> Hide them from sight so completely,
> That the world will never half-dream.
> Fashion the strong box securely.
> Then sit on the lid and laugh.[53]

I did as she suggested and buried my heartache. My mission in Shanghai was to continue to upgrade and expand RCA's network in China while signing up new customers. It was also an opportunity to prove my worth to RCA. I *had* to sit on the lid and laugh.

When I walked down the gangplank in Yokohama, old familiar smells assaulted me—tar, salt, brine, and the acrid smell of too many people. I pulled on my hat so the breeze wouldn't grab it and drop it at the feet of a black-clad porter pulling a cart. My linen suit was freshly laundered, my shoes polished. I carried one valise. I hadn't brought much because I planned to purchase custom suits and shoes when I settled in. They were dirt cheap, and I liked looking professional.

I spotted George Shecklen in the crowd on the dock wearing a pith helmet.

"Sheck, nice to see you." I hailed, raising my arm so he could spot me. After elbowing through the crowd, I said, "It's good to see a familiar face. What's with the pith helmet?"

"It certainly wouldn't blow away like your hat is trying to do. Besides, you never know what might come flying your way."

I gave my hat another tug and made a mental note to pick up a helmet.

"Street," he continued, "it's good to see you, too. It's been a while," and he pumped my hand. "You know that I have the utmost confidence in your ability to hold down the job, even though, at times, you will find it a tough one."[54]

"Thanks," I said. "It's nice to be back, Sheck. We've got catching up to do."

"We'll hop the train to Tokyo, and I'll fill you in during the ride. I've only got a couple of weeks before I head stateside."

Yokohama had grown since I'd last been there in 1919. The parlor where I'd gotten my tattoo was gone. Just as well. I laughed and showed my scar to Sheck.

When I told him my story, he shook his head and said, "Street, cover that thing up. I'm surprised the Navy let you in with that thing on your arm."

"They were desperate for radiomen."

"Must have been," he chuckled. "Well, you'll be working with a different crowd now. Before I leave, I will personally introduce you to my contacts. Are you up for introductions today? When we get to Tokyo, we can take the subway to most of our appointments."

"Subway? When was that built?"

"It opened in 1927. It's called the Tokyo Metro Ginza Line, and it stops at several wards with trolley and bus connections to just about every part of Tokyo. It makes getting around easy. I use it all the time."

"Last time I was here, rickshaws and carriages were the way to go."

After dinner with a client at Frank Lloyd Wright's Imperial Hotel, we spent the night in luxurious rooms and boarded the train for Kobe in the morning. There we spent a day meeting clients, and on the tenth of January, 1931 took a ship to Shanghai, my base of operations for China. The following day, after more introductions, we took two days to get to Hong Kong for a whirlwind day of meetings. Our last stop before returning to Shanghai was Manila, Territory of the Philippines, the headquarters for RCA in the Orient.

While we toured, Shecklen briefed me on the political and business hotbed I was stepping into. I had brushed up on the political history of China before I departed Oakland, but libraries left a lot to be desired. I read that the Qing rulers had lost their grip on China when they ceded treaty ports and relinquished their Korean colony to Japan. Now, Japan controlled vast sections of China's infrastructure—railroads, electricity, and radio. Uprisings swept the country. Men were cutting off their braided queues in protest.

Sheck filled in the blanks. "The *de facto* ruler of any province in China could be Chiang Kai-shek's Republic of China, the communists, or a local warlord. You will be working with all of them. In the International District in Shanghai—consisting of Britain, the United States, France, and Japan—citizens and economic interests are protected by each country's army and naval presence."

"I understand the International Settlement is run by a foreign-controlled council, primarily the British. As a radioman, I was advised to not wander too far from the settlement. Is that still the case?"

"That was good advice then, and it's better advice now," Sheck said. "Chinese politics and Japanese interference make the American radio project appear as creeping imperialism, not a popular concept these days. I've introduced you to RCA's main clients. Stick to business and keep your opinions to yourself. Watch your back, George."

Passport visa for China *(George Street Archive)*

chapter 10

Shanghai Revisited

1931
Shanghai

That afternoon, Sheck and I walked the length of the Bund— the promenade along the Huangpu River—on our way to the office, unable to converse over the noise. Boats powered by poles, sails, or propellers congested the waterway. Flat-bottomed sampans and every sort of houseboat clustered along the edges of the Bund packed

Along the Bund (*George Street Archive*)

so closely they formed a walkable seafront. Cars dodged rickshaws, some of them bicycle-driven instead of foot-pulled. Pedestrians, dressed in traditional and Western garb, lugged handcarts loaded with supplies.

I snapped a picture of a woman pushing a claw foot tub strapped to a trolley, the tub as big as she. A six-year-old beggar girl with hair bobbed like Bar-bara's clopped alongside me and gave my coat a tug.

Woman pushing a handcart *(George Street Archive)*

"Mis'wer, Mis'wer, you wat'chee," she implored. She skipped before me and then walked backward, juggling three large knives.

"Amazing, amazing," I told her, wishing I spoke the language so I could say more. I gave her a dime as a reward and bowed, grateful she had stopped. She followed us grinning from ear to ear until we turned the corner. On Avenue Prince Edward VII, four or five lanes wide, we ran into a group of tumblers holding up traffic with a sidewalk circus![55] Cars tried to hug the middle lane while pedestrians scrambled through the performers. People spilled into the roadway, forcing us to elbow through the throng. Fortunately, Sheck's pith helmet was easy to spot as I followed behind him.

We finally entered RCA's office in the Sassoon building, which also housed the Cathay Hotel. Sheck booked a room for me on his expense account until I could arrange less expensive accommodations.

"Boy, what a luxury after the ship's cramped quarters," I told Sheck. "This building wasn't here in 1919."

"Your right," Sheck said, "Sir Victor Sassoon, the building's designer, rode on the coattails of China's desire to be on parity with the West. He has developed several art deco hotels in the area."

The Bund, Shanghai 1931 *(George Street Archive)*

"He sounds like someone whose business we'd like to corner," I responded, thinking I could introduce myself and possibly arrange a runner to his hotels.

Sheck nodded in agreement and said, "How about going to the Canidrome for dinner and a show tonight? We might see him there. Nellie Farren's Coquettes are really something. They line up and dance in step with one another. Their costumes are pretty skimpy. And you can dance with a Russian for a price."

"I'm game. There was nothing like that the last time I was here. Let me clean up, and I'll meet you in the lobby."

In less than an hour, we hopped a trolley and headed for the Canidrome, which also housed the race track. We passed the newly completed Nanking Theatre and the Casanova dance hall on Avenue Prince Edward VII. I made a mental note to check them out later.

Shanghai was the same, and it was different from my steam schooner days. This time, I examined everything through the eyes of a businessman instead of those of a radioman looking for a bit of R&R. Roads were paved. Two-story buildings were now six stories or higher. Chinese families ambled in the public garden on the north end of the Bund. It had been closed to them last time I was here—had been since 1890. The pavilion and tennis courts were still there, but there were more benches.

When we arrived at the Canidrome, I was back in San Francisco. The ballroom was huge and resplendent. The stage featured a live band playing a type of jazz that was foreign to me.

"What are they playing?" I asked Sheck. "It's not half bad."

"From what I understand, it's unique to Shanghai. What you've got is a mix of classically trained White Russians, Filipinos, and American musicians playing pieces written by Chinese composers. Wait till you see the floor show."[56]

Russian women in fancy dress cruised the tables, offering to dance for a fee. After a few stiff drinks, I took a turn with one of the taxi dancers. She reminded me of Kay. She'd bleached her hair blond and tilted her head in the same coy way. Through the fog of smoke that hung like the mist on the Marin Headlands, I imagined Kay in my arms again. When the music stopped, I was sorry. I paid her, and then she was gone.

When I returned to our table, the lights dimmed, the music loudened, and the curtain rose from the stage at the head of the dance floor. Women in bras, garter belts, and feathers kicked up their heels like can-can girls and moved in unison, resembling an articulated snake. The floor show knocked my socks off, and we stayed for two. We left in the morning hours and took a rickshaw back to the Cathay Hotel, unconcerned about not meeting Sassoon.

Relaxing into the rickshaw seat, I sat back, closed my eyes, and listened to the heartbeat of the wickedest city in the East. The barking-dog sound of English like a band's percussion section, mixed with the tonal music of the Chinese language. Sailors, Chinese laborers, British council members, taxi dancers, policemen, and prostitutes babbled away. I let the symphony of humanity seep me away.

Sheck said, "Two million people are packed like sardines in a tin in Shanghai's nine-square miles."

I smiled. "Now there were two million and one, and that is okay. I'm happy I'm here."

When we arrived at the hotel, I thanked Sheck for a delightful evening, climbed the stairs with hat in hand, and fell asleep to the rhythms of the city.

The next day over lunch at the hotel restaurant—we'd missed breakfast—I asked Sheck about Little Russia and the refugees. The taxi dancer I'd met the night before haunted me.

"They're the White Russians who fled the Bolshevik revolution. When the commies took over, they killed and destroyed anyone and everything that had supported the Czar. People fled in droves, and Shanghai welcomed them. It's a treaty port, a haven. Jews and Greeks have fled here too."

"I remember reading something about it in the papers. Didn't the Soviet regime strip the refugees of citizenship, making them stateless?"

"Yes, that's exactly what happened. The League of Nations created the Nansen Passport so they could at least have identification. It's restrictive. A lot of countries won't recognize it."

"That's rough. They really are stuck."

"Women can get out if they marry someone with a passport. You gotta keep your wits about you; single women are always on the hunt."

"Are they destitute?" I asked, wondering about the taxi dancer I'd held in my arms.

"The first to flee escaped with money. They built an impressive Russian Orthodox Church in their Little Russia community. From what I've heard about a fifth of the Russian females are prostitutes. Dancing for a fee only goes so far, especially if there's a family to feed."

"They're beautiful women. Can't they find work in Europe?" I asked.

"Some do. A lot of documentation is required if they want to go to another country. There about fifty-thousand refugees in Shanghai, and the city has more prostitutes per capita than anywhere else in the world." [57]

"Wow"

"Street, there is nothing but sad stories when it comes to the Russian gals."

American Consulate	- Me Kuo Ling Tse Kou	花 棋
International Club	- Ku Chee Lian Huan Chia	國 際
Ministry of Communication	- Chiao Tung Pu	交 通
Ministry of Foreign Affairs	- Wai Chiao Pu	外 交
National Construction Comission	- Chiea Shih Wei Yua	
Yangtse Hotel	- Yangtze King Va Tiea	楊子江 飯店
Bridge House Hotel	- Wei Jong Va Tiea	惠龍飯店
National Aviation Office	Hong Koong Kung Sze (Sai T add.	
Military Flying Field	- Fi Chi Zan	飛機場
Shanghai-Nanking Railway Station	- Hsia Kwan Hu Cho S	
Radio Office (Inside Wall Nanking)	- Ku Ee Lang	逝 終

Cheat Sheet *(George Street Archive)*

Sheck then handed me a sheet of Chinese ideograms and their Romanized pronunciations so I could get from point A to point B.

"Keep this with you at all times," he said." "Point to the ideograms if you are not understood. I use mine all the time."

I folded it, slipped it into my wallet, and pulled out money for our lunch.

"I got this, Street. I'll put this on my expense account. You'll have one too, soon enough." He paid the bill, speaking to the waiter in Shanghainese, a mixture of English smattered with Japanese, French, and Mandarin. I patted my cheat sheet, thankful for the aid.

American club, Shanghai 1931
(George Street Archive)

While at RCA's headquarters in Manila, my supervisor advised me to join the American, French, and Columbia Country Clubs in Shanghai. I applied at each one as we made the rounds. All accepted me. Sheck recommended that I take a furnished room at the American Club and move out of the hotel. Clients would be close at hand. It was an impressive building, six stories high, close to the Bund, and made of concrete in the Georgian colonial style typical of America. It could have been in Seattle, Oakland, or San Francisco. Dark wood polished the interior billiard room and bars, but the architect designed the Mahjong room on the second floor with a Chinese coffered ceiling and decorated the walls with colorful paintings and lanterns. I anticipated conducting business over whiskey and cigars with the expatriates who congregated there.

Sheck and I ended our week cruising the *Casanova, Vienna Gardens,* and *Del Montes*, the neon-lit cabarets where Nanking Road becomes Bubbling Well Road. Girls, primarily Russians, performed impromptu floor shows if there were sufficient paying customers. I liked how they kicked up their heels but at the same time, felt sorry for them.

The day before, Sheck had handed me *the North-China Daily News* saying, "Street, read that editorial by Sir Percival Phillips. It's about the Russian girls you seem so fond of."

Percival reported that initially, the Russian girls, the "refugees from Manchuria, young girls, mothers, and even grandmothers who fought time with rouge and lipstick," had a monopoly as taxi dancers. In shimmering silk sheaths, Chinese girls now danced with lonesome partners for a fee, and "...the forlorn remnants of the sad Russian brigade... were hardly ever taken on the floor," which, of course, meant that they moved on to less desirable employment.[58]

After I finished reading without comment, Sheck said, "I need to take you to a Sing-Song restaurant. Then your education about Shanghai women will be complete."

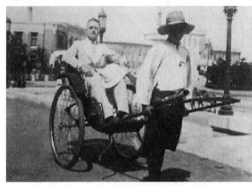

George Street in rickshaw, Shanghai.
(George Street Archive)

We headed to Foochow Road, frequented by wealthy Chinese. When we entered the tea house, the pungent smell of Chinese Five Spice and tobacco hung in the air. Men puffing on pipes sat with meticulously groomed courtesans with etched red lips and plucked brows. Wearing high-collared, side-slit silk sheaths that hugged their slim figures, the women entertained their guests in private booths—singing, reciting, playing music, or engaging in card games or Mahjong.

The proprietor came to our table and offered us a chit.

Sheck explained, "You fill out the chit for a Sing-Song girl. You can request one by name if you want or by age. Some are as young as fifteen. She will arrive like a queen in a bicycle rickshaw."

"Then what?" I asked.

"A romance might ensue after several meetings when the customer and the girl get to know one another. Meanwhile, money pours into the restaurant owner's coffers and the Sing-Song girl's purse."

We filled out a chit, and soon a young girl came to our booth. We enjoyed a game of cards with her. She could tell we were not serious clients, so she relaxed and enjoyed herself. We made sure to buy lots of tea.

chapter 11

Honorary Advisor

1931
China

The next day Sheck explained that he'd succeeded in developing a relationship with Chiang Kai-shek, the head of the Nationalist Party, which gained control of eastern China after his army ousted the Chinese Communists in 1927. Chiang Kai-shek's National Reconstruction Commission approached RCA about bringing wireless technology to Asia. Soon, he and President Hoover exchanged their first official messages from the newly opened Chengdu transmitting station which allowed for direct service between Shanghai and San Francisco.[59]

Sheck said, "Things were going good between RCA and Manchuria until Zhang Zuolin, Manchuria's ruling warlord and a rival of Chiang Kai-shek's, invited us to expand wireless into his territory. I talked to Chiang Kai-shek and reassured him that we recognized his government as having exclusive authority over radio. So I went ahead and signed a contract with Zuolin since he controlled Manchuria."

"How did Chiang Kai-shek take that? I asked.

"Well, it wasn't a problem for long. The Japanese Kwangtung Army assassinated Zuolin. By doing so, they inadvertently consolidated Chiang Kai-shek's authority over Manchuria and our position with him. Chiang Kai-shek honored the contract we had signed with Zuolin."

"The stars certainly aligned with you in that dicey situation," I said.

"Yes, indeed. I became an official advisor for communications, and the approval for a Shanghai-San Francisco circuit sailed like a hot knife cutting through butter."

"Why did Japan's army assassinate Zuolin?" I said, seeking confirmation of what I assumed I understood about Manchurian politics.

"As you probably know, southern Manchuria is Japan's breadbasket because Japan does not have sufficient resources to support its population. Japan controlled the Southern Manchurian Railroad and invested resources in Manchuria's infrastructure to facilitate the shipment of tons of food, steel, oil, and glass from Port Arthur to their home islands. They were unhappy when Zoulin was defeated at Peiping, [60] and Manchuria's economy tanked."

"Humm, doesn't make a whole lot of sense given the consequence."

"I think they expected to fill the power vacuum, not Chiang Kai-shek. The Japanese army is like a cobra without a charmer. It strikes where it wants before obtaining consent."

Sheck added, "Beware."

"I will. Will you be available for consultations if I get in a mess?"
I asked.

"Yes, but now that you know the ropes. I think you'll do fine.
The last thing I need to do before I leave for Manila is get you a
Power of Attorney for RCA, so you have the authority to sign
contracts."

I got to work after seeing Sheck off, pith helmet in hand and my
white linen suit pressed. I sized up the situation as being "one of
patience unending with plenty of perseverance required."[61]

George Street with pith helmet. *(George Street Archive)*

First, I tactfully organized the Chinese Government Radio
Administration central office to elevate service levels to standard

practices. That meant creating a modern, nationwide, long-distance network to increase traffic over our Shanghai-San Francisco and Shanghai-Manila circuits.

Japan's official protest against Chiang Kai-shek's government in Nanking delayed some of my work. The Japanese did not want direct wireless service between China and America. Headlines in the *Seattle Times*, *Chicago Tribune*, and *New York Times* stirred the pot: **"China-US Radio Draws Protest of Japan to Nanking."**[62]

In truth, Japan did not need to worry. China was mired in a maze of bureaucratic affiliations and way behind in radio technological know-how.

My report to Manila summarized the situation:

> None of the officials, except the Minister, have a great deal of authority when it comes to financial expenditures, even in small amounts. Generally, requests for expenditures for spare parts, advertising, etc., pass up the ladder from General Manager Chang to Director Lu and, if approved, then to Nanking.
>
> I also organized the Commercial Department consisting of four young Chinese men. They had no telegraph or radio experience; their only qualification was that they could speak English. Of the four Commercial Representatives, one is showing results, another one is fair, and two are next to useless. One American can accomplish more than the lot of them in a single day.[63]

I tackled the domestic system next with more than just radio in mind. I was aware that I must only drink boiled water and add a teaspoon of potassium permanganate to my bathwater to kill the stuff in Shanghai water. But I was not prepared for a public facility that sold toilet paper for a copper per sheet. According to the sign, purchasing was not compulsory!

The domestic radio system in Shanghai was as pitiful as the public facilities. It consisted of rare pieces of equipment that only the junkman in the U.S. would handle. Given the tools, moving traffic beyond Shanghai was truly remarkable. When I got the system beyond the Dark Ages, I assisted with the first voice tests on a radio-telephone between Shanghai and San Francisco.[64] In April 1931, R.R. Beal spoke to Mr. Slater using the Bolinas transmitters in California.

On 25 June 1931, I was appointed Honorary Advisor of the Minister of Communications, National Government of China. The *China Press* announced my new position on the front page along with news about beheaded vampires, star-struck actresses, and the goings-on in Little Russia.[65] I sent a clipping to Ma so she could share it with Georgie and Barbara and included money so she could buy them a little something from their lonesome dad. Honestly, I was so busy I had little time for reflection. By now, my job consisted of circuit supervisor, service clerk, operator if needed, equipment repairman, pricing, complaint settler, and solicitor.

For the first time, traffic *from* China to San Francisco exceeded that of San Francisco *to* China. In my report to E. J. Nally, I requested an additional man and passed on a request from China's Director of the Bureau of International Telegraphs for a hundred thousand dollar loan to improve their domestic stations.[66]

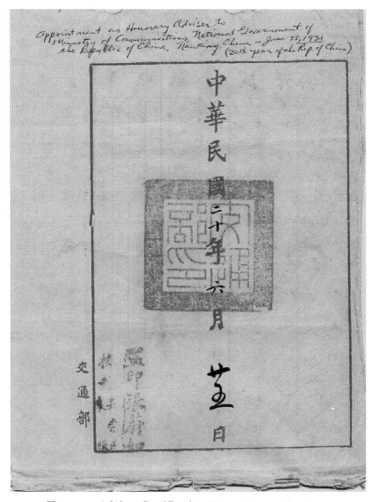

Honorary Advisor Certification *(George Street Archive)*

Then in August, I flew to Peiping to connect Chiang Kai-shek's radio network to the world. From there, I traveled eighty miles to Tientsin, then north to Manchuria. I linked Manchuria's and China's major cities to Nanking along the way. In Mukden (Shenyang), I flipped the switch that connected Manchuria to San Francisco. The August 21st edition of the *North Star China News* announced: **Radio Now links China Directly with the World.**

That same month, a flood of Biblical proportions poured down the Yangtze River. It inundated five hundred square miles. Half a million people had to abandon their homes and farms.

I witnessed the destruction on my way to Peiping from Shanghai aboard a military Junkers aircraft. Flying in the Junkers was like being in a corrugated tin can. It was noisy, cold, and bouncy. I white-knuckled it the whole way, hoping like hell I wouldn't become another body floating in the river that had become an inland sea.

George pulling a rickshaw in front of Yamato Hotel, Mukden
(*George Street Archive*)

Not surprisingly, the Japanese objected to the Manchuria link, which created a dilemma for me and RCA since the Japanese market was as important to us as the Chinese market. The Japanese filed a formal protest, and I had to figure out how to negotiate my way through this delicate labyrinth. Patience, deference, and a letter from New York smoothed ruffled feathers.

In Mukden, Manchuria, a city trying to catch up to the modern world, I got a big kick out of a sign set along a roadside and snapped a picture. It read:

```
        No fowling-piece allowed [shot gun]
               No plucking allowed
          No fishing or hunting allowed
          No clamor or quarrel allowed
               No burning allowed
     No throwing from the elevated allowed
              No nakedness allowed
          No urine outside W.C. allowed⁶⁷
```

The Japanese would have been happy to see a ninth rule added: No Chinese allowed.

I met an Associated Press correspondent during a stopover in Harbin, Manchuria. He was also a telephone teacher and installer for the Automatic Telephone Co. of Chicago, a company trying to get a foothold in Asia. While walking with him to a restaurant, he spotted a handbill on a telephone post.

Harbin, 1931 GS at the reins.
(George Street Archive)

"Street, give me a minute to decipher this," Mitchell said. It was in Chinese ideographs, which I couldn't read. I stopped and listened to him mumble. Then he pushed back his hat, looked me in the eye, and said, "Things [are] getting hot between China and Japan. I expect that trouble will break out any day now…"[68]

"Really, any day now?" I asked, stunned.

"Yes, it would be wise to return to Shanghai as soon as possible. I don't want to be around when the shooting starts." Over a quick meal, we kicked around scenarios and arranged for a flight. I couldn't help but wonder how things would play out and how it would affect my mission.

chapter 12

From Russia with Love

1931
China

Before Sheck left, he gave me some practical advice, "watch your step in playing with those Russians too heavily. It is easy to overstep, and reputations are easily made (bad ones, I mean). Get yourself a couple of good white mamas and leave the Slavs alone."[69]

He never met Nina. In September, I did—at a nightclub in Tsingtao (Qingdao), a port north of Shanghai on the Yellow Sea. I was on a stopover from Dalian.

After the floor show, she had approached me.

"You want dance again?" she asked. "You pay good."

"You look familiar. Were you at the Canidrome?" I asked.

"Yes, I taxi dancer, sometimes."

"I remember you," I said. She was the one who reminded me of Kay. She danced like Kay, too, brushing against me and then twirling away. Our vibrations were strong. I was like a receiver, tuned to the emotions bombarding my senses. Nina was the transmitter. With a look, she could get a rise out of me.

"How old are you?" I asked as I led her to the dance floor. She had the rounded face of youth yet it was etched with experience. She was younger than me, for sure.

"I twenty-three. Been here ten years. My name Nina."

She told me her story when we returned to the table for drinks.

"My family White Russians. My father like Czar. We had money, nice house in Vladivostok. I learn English at school. Communists make riots. Murder Czar and family in cold blood. Red army murder White Russians. My father put sister and me on train for Little Russia. I thirteen. My sister older."

"Only thirteen? You must have been terrified. Did you ever hear from your parents again?"

"No. All I got is picture. My brother too young. I never see again. They killed."

I reached across the table and took her hands. What a plight for one so young. My heart ached for her. She went on to explain, in her halting English, that after she and her sister reached Shanghai, they made their way to Little Russia and sought refuge. Destitution was their motivator. They and the other students they had traveled with formed an "entertainment troupe," a euphemism that could mean just about anything in Shanghai. Within a short period of time, a British soldier married her sister. Her sister left for England once she obtained her passport, and Nina was on her own.

"I survive," she said. She needed no other words. She may look like Kay, but she was no pampered princess. And I liked that about her.

After more drinks and flings around the dance floor, she asked, "You want private floor show? I make happy," and she glanced at my crotch. I embarrassed myself by following her gaze and readily agreed.

We made our way to my room, arm-in-arm. I wasn't with business associates, so I was comfortable escorting her up the stairs. In the morning, I wanted more of this woman from Little Russia, and we arranged to meet again.

I brought Nina back to Shanghai, registering her as Mrs. Street when we booked her a room. I gave her spending money, but kept her at a discrete distance. It was safer for a young man of thirty-four, and more acceptable, to keep a woman rather than risk the consequence of pleasures purchased at the red light district. One notorious prostitute had cut off the penis and testicles of her "lover" and carried them around in her purse. Word got around, and I took notice.

Nina stepping on George's foot c. 1931
(George Street Archive)

When I walked into RCA's central office after settling Nina, I had to make accrediting arrangements with the Chinese National Telegraph for the bevy of American newspaper reporters traveling upriver to Nanking. They were here to cover Charles and Anne Lindbergh's "North to the Orient" trip, the first time anyone flew west to east via the Great Circle Route.[70]

Since I shared an office with the Chinese Government Radio Administration (CGRA), getting the needed documents was easy. As their Honorary Advisor, I recommended they contact Lindbergh's plane by radio when they flew in from Japan. It would be good publicity. I told the supervisor that he need to ask Shanghai's central transmitting and receiving stations to use two transoceanic transmitters keyed simultaneously to different frequencies in order to reach the Lindberghs.

At 9:00 AM on September 19th, I sat at an operators position and, in International Morse Code, started calling Lindbergh's plane at K6CAL. I set a slow speed. I'd read that Mrs. Lindbergh held an amateur's radio license and was to act as the radio operator for their transpacific flight. After twenty minutes, I made contact.

"We have been answering you since you first called," keyed Mrs. Lindbergh

"Then please QRQ" (send faster), I keyed.

"QRX" (stand by)

Minutes passed. Then she keyed, "Can you give us a weather report, please?"

That made me pause. At the time, the only weather station was in the French Concession, at either a monastery or church. Telephoning there, I discovered the weatherman did not work Saturdays. What to do? I had flown a couple of times between Shanghai and Nanking on the flying boats of the Chinese National Airlines, so I knew what kind of information Lindbergh needed.

I hoofed it to the second floor of the Sassoon Building, taking the steps two at a time, and stuck my head out a window. I observed the roof line of the Bank of China building across the street on Jiukeo

Road, guessed its height, and then multiplied that to determine the final altitude to the base of the overcast.

I got back on the radiotelegraph key to K6CAL and reported, "Shanghai has no official weather stations. Present weather overcast. Ceiling about five hundred feet. If you can find the river's main course, follow it one hundred ninety miles until you come to a round hill called Purple Mountain. That is Nanking." [71]

I waited for a response but was interrupted by a Chinese staff member who handed me a note. It was from RCA-San Francisco. "Do you know what is with Mukden? It has been ZOA (off the air) since 2:00 AM." I relayed that I would try and find out. I called the Chinese Radio Service and was told, "We are not working with them right now."

How to find out what was going on in Mukden? I knew news offices had stringers—freelance journalists—located just below the Great Wall on the border with Manchuria, where the railroad ran through a breach in the wall. If I could confirm that no passenger trains were running, I would know something was up. I called every newsagent I could think of—Reuters, my friend Mitchell at the Associated Press, and the New York Times. No answers. They were all in Nanking awaiting the Lindberghs. Then McEwan from the United Press picked up.

"I thought you were in Nanking," I said

"No, I have a cold, so I sent my assistant."

"Mukden has gone offline, and I'm trying to figure out what is going on," I told him.

"If you'll be in the office for a while, I can come over."

"Come on," I said. "I'm not going anywhere."

Five minutes later, in walked McEwan. We sent an urgent message to his office in Tientsin and waited an hour. Then we received a news flash, "Trains, freight cars, flatcars jammed with people leaving Mukden. Japan's Kwangtung Army in action."

McEwan sent a wireless to United Press and got a six-hour lead on the Manchurian Incident. Japan's army had blown apart their own railroad claiming the Chinese had done it so they could justify a war!

Meanwhile, the evening edition of the *Shanghai Evening Post & Mercury* ran a story about how the Chinese Government Radio Administration had established contact with Colonel Charles Lindbergh. "Talking to Shanghai by radio 1:23 this afternoon, Colonel Lindbergh asked for a weather report from CGRA, which CGRA officials promptly furnished."[72] I was pleased. There's nothing like free publicity, and I went up a notch in the eyes of the CGRA.

But there was nothing in the news about Manchuria—yet.

The Japanese army marched across Manchuria, damaging our antennas and equipment. Our radio links went quiet, and I wired the news to San Francisco.

I took a moment to write Ma because undoubtedly she would worry when the news hit the papers. I played down the severity of the situation. I wrote that there was nothing much new or exciting except the war in Manchuria. All I said about it was, "I suppose you will see it in your papers." Then I filled in the rest of my letter with, "I don't feel so hot. Hope to stay away from hospitals...Santa Claus seems to be creeping up again. I am enclosing $20.00 American Express checks payable to you. I will be grateful if you will use it to buy something for George Jr. and Barbara....Maybe they need new overcoats or shoes or something. If this doesn't cover what they need in that way, please tell me."[73]

After a quiet Thanksgiving of duck instead of turkey and no contact with our Mukden station, I traveled to Peiping to suggest the traffic centers for domestic and international radio services merge to expedite service. The Chinese liked the idea but asked, "Where do we get the money?" The Japanese invasion of Manchuria and the Great Yangtze flood had sapped their resources. I reported the situation to headquarters, concluding, "In spite of the various hindrances, we have enjoyed close contact and cooperation with all of the officials, which is very necessary and which is resulting in a mutual increase of revenue."[74]

By the end of November, Sheck had returned from his extended leave, and officially my assignment was over. But Japan's continued protests against RCA needed fixing. To unruffle feathers, RCA asked me to go to Japan. It was another six months of income. I wrote to Ma so she could break the news that Daddy wasn't coming home for Christmas.

chapter 13

The Land of the Rising Sun

December 15, 1931
Japan

Hon. Wang Peh-chun,
Minister of Communications,
National Government of the Republic of China.
Nanking.
Honorable Sire:

> This letter is to advise you that my employers have called upon me to leave China and take up duty elsewhere. Accordingly, I am sailing away on 16 December [1931] for Tokyo.
>
> I beg to express my whole hearted appreciation of the close cooperation and support that I have enjoyed from the Ministry of Communications, the Bureau of International Telegraphs and the Chinese Government Radio Administration. It has

been a great deal of pleasure that I have been designated to act as Honorary Advisor in the absence of Mr. George F. Shecklen who, as you undoubtedly know, recently returned from his holiday.

I feel that radio communications from China to the outside world and within China will continue to expand and prosper rapidly which will be of material benefit to your Ministry and to the Chinese people as a whole.

Wishing you, Honorable Sire, a happy and prosperous new year.

Sincerely yours,
George Street
Representative.[75]

About the same time as my transfer, I found out RCA's vice president, W. A. Winterbottom, planned an inspection tour with his wife in tow. Apparently, there wouldn't be a sale of RCA-Communications after all. I was to accompany them in Japan after Sheck hosted them in China. I'd have to hustle since I had little time to prepare.

Our success at expanding China's network prompted Winterbottom to reorganize the Radio Corporation of the Philippines into an RCA-Communication branch office, which increased traffic efficiency between San Francisco, Asia, Berlin, Madrid, and Geneva. When he completed his task, he hosted a luncheon that brought all the communications representatives together, including the

Philippine Government Department of Communications and U. S. military radio department heads.

Things were moving fast, and I hadn't told Nina about my transfer. Nina stayed at a boarding house when we weren't traveling together. Fortunately, her house mistress was good about ignoring her whereabouts as long as she paid the rent on time, which I occasionally helped with.

I called Nina to break the news, and she agreed to meet me in my room at the American Club.

Inhaling her scent, I pulled her to me as soon as she stepped across the threshold. Then I held her at arm's length and stared into her eyes. There was no sense in delaying the inevitable. I said, "Nina, I'm sorry to have to tell you this. RCA has reassigned me to Tokyo. Japan complained to the right people. They feel slighted about RCA expanding China's wireless network. I'll be in Japan for several months."

"What, you leave me? What I do? I mean nothing to you?" she said in her broken English.

"You do, Nina. But I have to go."

"Quit job and be with me,"

"Nina, you know I can't do that. What would I do in China? How could I make enough to care for you and still send money to Kay? You must see that."

"To hell with Kay and kids. My father no send money. I survive."

"You'll survive again. It's one of the things I like about you."

"Only one? You miss me."

"Yes, I will miss you," and I pulled her tight as she continued to rant. I wanted to take her with me. I enjoyed her companionship, and the sex was great—transformative and glistening. She also knew how to be discreet, unlike Kay. She filled the void of loneliness that crept into the quiet hours—those times when I longed for my children and the touch of those who loved me.

"Nina, I have to leave on the sixteenth. I wish you could come."

"True?" she asked, pulling away from me so she could look into my eyes." You want me come?"

"Yes," I said, and I grasped her hands and nodded.

"I figure out way," Nina said. "I have year on Nansen passport. I just renew. I travel to Japan for work."

"That might work, my little street smart, Nina. You must get a visa on your own. I can't sponsor you or hire you. I hope you can make it happen," I replied, knowing that if anyone could make such a bold move, Nina could. By the time I left for Japan, Nina was well on her way to receiving a work visa.

When I arrived in Tokyo, I settled into the Imperial Hotel while I got the lay of the land. I got on the waiting list for a western-style apartment and began meeting RCA's existing clients. On the first of January, I flew by airplane from Tokyo to Osaka, then hopped the train to Kobe. Along the way, I stopped at Kyoto, Nara, and Nagoya to visit clients and prepare for Winterbottom's tour.

While in Kyoto, an associate took me to the famous geisha district of Gion. "Do you think I should take Winterbottom here? " I asked.

"Probably not, especially since his wife will be with him. Reserve this for clients as you did with Sing-song girls in China." Then he said, "Be sure you don't have holes in your socks. You'll be doing a lot of business in your stocking feet. There are no shoes allowed in most Japanese establishments."

I admit I was taken aback. I prided myself in how I dressed, well aware that a person had only one shot at a good first impression. I had fewer suits than some, but they were well cut, custom made, as were my shoes, and I always wore a freshly laundered shirt. Ma used to chide, "You never know when you might end up in the hospital, and you'd be so embarrassed if you had holes in your underwear."

Consequently, I never ever wore holey socks or underwear. As a matter of fact, Kay used to complain about my spending too much time dressing. She'd say, "You primp as much as a woman," which did not sit well with me. Nina doesn't mind. She liked "Dapper Dan" on her arm.

It was one of those magical Kyoto nights when the sky glowed cherry-blossom pink in the setting sun as we headed to the Gion district. We settled ourselves in a rickshaw to go to the Ichiriki Tea House, the most exclusive in Japan's oldest city. My associate and I were to meet a government administrator who was a welcome guest at that particular tea house. When our driver lowered his poles so we could exit, he bowed and smiled as though he was honored to have pulled our heavy Western bodies to such a fine establishment. I stepped aside and glanced up and down the street just as a bicyclist raced by, cranking his metal bell in warning. Paper lanterns cast soft warmth on the boardwalk illuminating the entrances of a warren of wood establishments, crushed together like rows of books. They had no yards or separating gardens. A breath of wind could have collapsed them like a line of dominoes.

The maid at the door of the establishment greeted me by name, "Street-san, you are expected. Please honor us with your presence." She helped us slip off our shoes, took our hats, and guided us through a polished wooden walkway. We passed a miniature landscape of such serenity that the street noise seemed to vanish. Incense and the smell of old wood engulfed me. Shadows stirred on shoji screen panels mystifying the surroundings. Our footfalls were silent as we made our way.

The maid opened a panel, bowed at the waist, and gestured for us to enter. It closed behind us with a soft grumble. Tatami mats lined the floor, defining the space and adding a hint of dust and straw to the pungent smell of pine. A hostess rose effortlessly from her kneeling position and directed us to a lacquered table with cushions on the floor for seating. I folded myself into an uncomfortable squat with my rear resting on my feet, wishing I was more flexible. She returned with saké while we waited for the minister. The hostess poured again when the minister was seated with his two geishas, paid for by my company. The hostess lit a one-hour incense stick to keep track of the geisha's time and would charge accordingly—the more sticks, the higher the bill.

It was the first time I had been close to geishas, and I must admit I was a bit unsettled. What was behind their white mask, slit with red lips? Fanciful combs adorned their black hair, piled into flawless folds. Their glistening silk kimonos, held tight with a wide obi, stiffened their posture. I smelled something like wet pebbles as they minced by on their tightly bound feet. My associate caught my questioning eye and said, "Before a geisha departs for the evening, a spark of flint is struck on her back for good luck."

He whispered, "The one with a red collar and the red lower lip is an apprentice, a Maiko, the "sister" of the geisha, still a virgin."

The geisha kept the conversation and saké flowing, directing her apprentice to pour while she subtly controlled the progression of the evening. Food magically appeared, deftly delivered by maids. At one point, another geisha entered with a shamisen, and the geisha and her apprentice danced, or should I say flowed in unison to the high-pitched notes plunked by the musician. The sound grated on my Western ears—tinny—yet sedate and without melody. The dancers dipped and turned and twisted their upper bodies, flashing fans coyly as they revealed the story behind the music. Sadness, delight, and stillness swept across their masked faces. Their kimonos shimmered and puddled at their feet like falling water. They reminded me of a silk painting that came to life, as delicate as the brushstrokes, as subtle as a Japanese garden. The power and beauty of their mystery had me eating out of their hands. I had difficulty remembering they were just women, not ethereal beings from an unknown universe. Concise, controlled, and ever courteous. Their confidence empowered and renewed me. I understood then and there the power of entertaining clients with geishas. I also sensed that Nina's jealousy would be ferocious!

When we bid farewell, the geishas escorted us to the door, helped us with our shoes, and bowed when we climbed into our rickshaw. I turned to my learned friend and said, "That was a first for me. I'd seen geishas when I was here as a radioman, but I took my pleasures elsewhere. Tell me what you know about geishas. My Western mind immediately associated them with women for hire. Did you ever lay with one?"

"No. Geishas are for looking, not touching. They are a business tool, a living commodity, and a precious jewel of the Japanese culture. Men bid for the privilege of taking a Maiko for the first time, driving the price into the thousands of yen. When their time comes, the Maiko don't allow kissing because of their makeup. They remain still not wanting to mess-up their hairdo, which they pay to have done once a week. Most geishas find a wealthy patron. If they are lucky, their patron called a Danna, will keep them for a lifetime. The Minister is probably the geisha's patron. If you want a romp, go across the river and find a prostitute. The Mama-san at the door will find a match for your pleasure."

"Do the geishas live with their patron?" I asked.

"No, not always," he replied with a grin. "They are the property of the owner of the geisha house, an okiya, where they trained. Their education in the arts—dance, music, and ceremony—is funded by the mother of the okiya and billed to the geisha. A patron pays off his geisha's debts, often buys her from the mother, and sets her up in a villa."

"So they are like indentured slaves or kept women?"

"Westerners don't have an equivalent. They are like rare gems stashed away for the exclusive use of the mother or patron. Their life is controlled, but they are revered like the Vestal Virgins of ancient Greece."

"Do they volunteer to be geishas?" I asked, feeling naïve.

"No, they are usually brokered to the okiya through an intermediary who buys them from desperate parents."

"My goodness that must be hard." I shook my head, suppressing my distaste, baffled by parents abandoning, selling or giving away their children.

"It is part of their culture. We must respect it," Sheck said.

I said I understood and asked about other tea houses where I could "rent" geishas, having experienced the power of their presence.

My associate named a couple, and I wrote them in the notebook I always carried in my pocket. He slapped me on the back, saying, "That's good business, George, good business, and you can expense it."

When Sheck finished my introductions, I departed Kyoto by train, rumbling past the rice paddies that washed the edges of rolling hills. The last time I was here, scores of people, up to their ankles in water, tended and planted the fields, their hands and feet prune-like by the end of the day. Men wore large-brimmed hats as they bent in half to plant the rice. The women protected their hair under tied bandanas. They were faceless in a sea of hunched backs, eking out a living, lost in the timeless struggle for survival. Now in the cold of winter, I wondered how many had sold their daughters to geisha and prostitution houses because of the Great Depression. I couldn't imagine doing such a thing to Barbara, having her taken away, losing control of her welfare. How could a mother abandon her child? How could a father endure such a thing?

I made a note to write Ma and tell her how grateful I was for her watchful eye. I'd write the children too.

12 March 1932

Dear Ma,

… Many thanks tho for your nice letters and your kindness to see my children so often. Am very glad to hear they are well and doing nicely….

Much love,

George

chapter 14

Little White Lies

1932
Japan

Once the Winterbottoms arrived in Tokyo in early January following their China tour, I became their guide. I arranged for a taxicab to meet us at the Imperial Hotel for the first day of our tour. "I'd like to go in a rickshaw," Winterbottom said.

"It will be quite bumpy where we're headed," I said, "Japan has neglected their roads, choosing instead to invest in their rail system."

"I think I'll stay," Mrs. Winterbottom said. "I like Frank Lloyd Wright's architecture and want to explore the hotel with its pillars of light. The park across the street looks appealing, too."

I assured her it was safe to go to the park alone, and Winterbottom and I settled into the cab. Our first stop was the RCA office in the Jiji building, not far from the Tokyo train station and the Imperial Palace. Next, we rumbled along the newly built Y-shaped Miyoshi Bridge to the Ginza district. Flat-bottomed boats floated the river tended by nimble-footed men.

"Ginza Street reminds me of San Francisco," Winterbottom remarked. Trolleys, buses, and cars crisscrossed in front of us. A well-dressed man in a suit and derby stooped to grab a piece of garbage. He tucked it in his pocket, apparently for later disposal. "So that's how they keep the streets clean," said Winterbottom. From then on, I did the same, picking up bits and putting them in my pocket.

"Would you like to get a glimpse of the Emperor?" I asked Winterbottom. "I read in the paper that he would depart his palace through the Sakuradomon Gate today. We could head that way and perhaps see him."

"Yes, let's go," he said. "I'll probably never have another opportunity like this."

I directed the driver, hoping we could see Japan's living deity. Traffic came to a crawl. Then, a loud explosion grabbed our attention as we descended the hill from the American Embassy.

"What was that?" Winterbottom asked. Smoke wisped across the moat and engulfed the guards surrounding the Emperor's carriage.

I stuck my head out the window. Attendants were grabbing horses' bridles to quiet them. "All I see is smoke and frightened horses," I responded, hoping my hare-brained idea hadn't landed us in the middle of a riot.[76]

We remained inside our cab at a standstill. More police converged on the area. I mopped my brow as time stretched. Finally, we eased forward. The Emperor was nowhere in sight, but blood splattered the road where he had been. Police hurried us through. It was impossible to ask questions amid the chaos. Given the circumstances and Japan's growing anti-American attitude, we proceeded without knowing what we had witnessed.

I later learned that a Korean had thrown a hand grenade under a carriage, hoping to kill the Emperor and end China's provisional rule over his country. The assassin disguised himself as a Kempeital military policeman to get close to the Emperor's entourage. His grenade missed its mark. It rolled under Imperial Household Minister Baron Ichiki Kitokuro's carriage killing his two horses, which explained the blood.

Winterbottom shared our adventure with his wife when we returned. She was aghast. After freshening up, the three of us headed to the Ginza district, reassuring Mrs. Winterbottom that all would be well. Ginza is a business district by day, but by nightfall, a cacophony of street merchants and peddlers hawk their wares until midnight. Winterbottom sat for a street artist and had his portrait done for next to nothing. It was later published in the RCA newsletter.[77]

RCA News, Vol. 13, Apr. 1932, p.9
(George Street Archive)

We hopped the train to Nagoya the next day to inspect our Yosami transmitting station. Mrs. Winterbottom joined us. We toured the facility with S. Shigehisa,

K. Yonemura, and Baron Togo.

IN FRONT OF YOSAMI TRANSMITTING STATION—FROM LEFT TO RIGHT· S. SHIGEHISA, K. YONEMURA, GEORGE STREET, MRS. W. A. WINTERBOTTOM, W. A. WINTERBOTTOM, F. AMANO, BARON TOGO

RCA News, Vol.13, April 1932, p. 6. *(George Street Archive)*

I'd barely seen Nina, who had accomplished a miracle and obtained a work visa so she could join me in Japan. She traveled by steamer. The ship had armed guards in the event of a pirate raid. Spiked steel bars separated the crew from the passengers. I settled her at the Imperial Hotel in a separate room and did not register her as Mrs. Street — no hanky-panky this time. Instead, we'd eye each other from across the room and kept our distance. I did not want to raise eyebrows, especially the Winterbottoms.

After days of luncheons, sightseeing, and meetings, the Winterbottoms finally left for Honolulu. Within days of their departure, rooms became available in the Bunk Apartments, Ochanomizu district, one of only two designed for foreigners. The flat was fully furnished with throw rugs, western-style furniture, and a regular bed instead of futons. Nina and I unpacked our bags and headed to the Asakusa Shopping Center, a twenty or thirty-minute taxi ride away, to buy basic necessities for our new home.

"I think I'll buy some gifts for the children," I said as we made our way through the crowded streets.

"Why you spend money?" Nina asked. "You send money to Kay?"

The cab pulled to a curb where small shops lined each side of the long street that ended at a temple. I paid the cabbie and continued our conversation when we stepped onto the pathway.

"Nina, I send money for their everyday expenses. I want to get them something special to remember me by and to let them know I'm thinking about them."

"They children. They no think about you. You spoil them, make them expect nice things. Not way to be," Nina retorted.

"Well, in my country, we give gifts to let people know we care about them. To show our love."

"You buy gifts for me because I *give* you love. How children pay you back?"

"Certainly not the same way," I said in jest. "We'll buy something for Ma, too. Something special."

"Geisha fan!" Nina said. "You buy me one, too, and I show you how use it right way."

I shook my head at her precociousness, imagining what she would do with one. People from around the world bartered with the merchants and spilled into the street. It was like seeing all of humanity in one place. Geisha floated by like flowers in a stream, their silk kimonos shimmering in spots of sunlight. We greeted steamer passengers who had stopped over for a day. I bought gifts to ship home despite Nina's protests. I sent Ma a large lacquered fan, hand-painted with flowers like the geisha use. I bought Barbara a parasol made of rice paper, and for George Jr., I got a calligraphy set along with a book of Japanese symbols. It had been over a year since I'd seen them. George Jr. was ten now, and Barbara would soon be eight.

I asked Nina, "Do you think they'll remember what I look like? It will be at least another year before I see them again. I hope Kay is taking good care of them."

"Yes, they remember. I sure grandmothers taking care of them," Nina responded. "They mothers. Georgie and Barbara lucky have so many mothers. Stop worry."

"Yes, *they will* remember, is how you say it. But you're probably right," I said as I gave Nina a squeeze, "They *are* fortunate to have so many mothers."

Nina's English was improving. I tried not to correct her English constantly, but her lack of prepositions and verbs drove me crazy. I reminded myself she hadn't had a mother to help her when she needed one, and her schooling had been interrupted. I appreciated the benefits she freely gave and delighted in the spice of our clandestine relationship. I guess I was her patron now, her Danna. Maybe the East and the West weren't that different after all. At least in the East, the geisha wasn't frowned upon. I'd have to buy her a kimono.

The following day, I lunched with potential clients at the Marunouchi Building near the Tokyo train station. I was one of six or seven foreigners who sat among a couple of hundred Japanese dressed in street kimonos topped with hard Derby hats. Securing a table for one or two was impossible. There was always one or more Japanese who joined us. Fortunately, the menu had English and French translations and numbered items. So, it was simple to order if you could read numbers in Japanese, ichi, ni, san, et cetera. If in doubt, I just pointed.[78]

After our meal and negotiations, I headed to the men's room but had not yet learned the symbols for Ladies' and Men's. My guest had departed, so I had no one to ask. As luck would have it, I entered the Ladies' room, where two women scrubbed the tile floor. They bowed. One said something in Japanese, and I turned to leave. She must have realized I did not understand, so she bowed again and said, "Dozo," She then walked over to a stall and held open the door for me. What a courtesy! After that, I learned the ideograph for men. Not that it makes any particular difference to the Japanese people. On the floor level of the railway station, the entrance to the toilets is a common one for all, with only low partitions dividing the large room in half.[79]

The Marunouchi Building also contained the barbershop I frequented because they cut Western hairstyles. One time, while I was seated awaiting my turn, six giant sumo wrestlers with long hair piled upon their heads joined me. The chairs overflowed with their bulk. I scooted over. An Englishmen next to me translated.

"They ordered the barber to shave off their hair," he said, and this created much "*yacha-machi*" (street talk) because the barber did not want to defile a long-standing custom by shearing off the locks of such brave men."

Then the barbers waved their scissors in the air. The wrestlers grabbed them and cut their hair while the barbers tried to snatch them back. I feared a riot. It quieted down after ten or fifteen minutes, and the barbers returned to work. I found out later the wrestlers were protesting something and had gone on strike. They wanted to show their dissatisfaction by shaving their heads.[80]

**

In late February, Nina and I found a beautiful villa in Kamakura, about forty miles south of Tokyo, overlooking the sea. I snapped it up and moved in immediately. I hopped a train to work. Nina did the shopping, cooked meals, and kept our villa spotless. In the evenings, we strolled the beach. I relished the relentless abandon of the churning ocean. I tried to capture it on film, but something was always missing—its enormity and sound, and its liquidness. As much as I loved our villa, something was missing, just like in my pictures of the sea. It was my children. I missed them and found that I was drawn to families enjoying their children.

George in Kamakura *(George Street Archive)*

One breathlessly warm night, we came across a people working on their fishing nets. They had hauled their sampan onto the beach and stretched their net across the sand. The husband was clothed in nothing more than a strip of loincloth. The woman was similarly clad. Their children had nothing on.[81]

"They're naked," I exclaimed. "Different countries, different customs, I guess," I said to Nina as the family bowed to us.

"What wrong with nakedness?" She asked. "You Americans so uneasy about body. Everyone have same bits and bobs. You... what the word? Ashamed. "

I couldn't think of an intelligent response, so I suggested, "Let's go home, and you can teach me all about being naked."

Nina gave me a coy look and teased, "I put on new kimono you give me first. Naked."

She was so different from Kay, who always teased and flirted but was stilted in bed. Nina taught me a thing or two about lovemaking, and I couldn't get enough of her. I couldn't help but wonder what Mother would think of Nina. I hadn't mentioned her in my letters. A mistress. Posing as Mrs. Street. Ma would faint.

Nina in kimono 1931
(George Street Archive)

chapter 15

Into the Fray

1932
Manchuria

The situation in Manchuria worsened, and Shanghai politics weren't much better. In Manchuria, the Japanese occupied and controlled communications, and conflict continued on the Eastern Railroad, which China and Russia owned.

China's leadership was disintegrating, and Japan was happy to fill the void—which worried RCA. How far would Japan expand its new boundary? Rumors rushed to fill the vacuum of uncertainty. The most concerning was Japan's planned take over our transmitting station at Chenju, about 600 miles from Shanghai. Memorandums from the Consul General of Shanghai to the U.S. Secretary of State spelled it out—expect a takeover at eight o'clock, January 25th.[82]

RCA Pacific Network 1932
(George Street Archive)

I read the news with growing concern, and, sure enough, a fleet of Japanese warships entered the Huangpu River, the primary access to the Bund and the French and International Settlements in Shanghai. Japanese marines patrolled the waterfront. In the old city section, an explosion shattered windows and killed twenty-nine. Small boats sank, and a Japanese soldier shot and killed an American Express employee.

Chinese troops sealed their quarter. The International (American and British) and French concessions also positioned their troops. If the Japanese entered their territories or harmed residents, they could intervene.[83] Chinese merchants appealed to their national government to end the terror that stalked the streets of Shanghai. The situation reminded me of cats trying to claw their way out of a bag.

On January 27th, U.S. Secretary of State Stimson asked the Consul General to inform the Japanese Consul General of the following:

> RCA had a substantial interest in the
> transmitting station at Chenju, that their
> Shanghai circuit carried a substantial portion
> of Chinese traffic which generates substantial
> income to RCA that the American government is
> seriously concerned and would greatly regret
> any interference with [the] channels of com-
> munication to and from Shanghai. The State
> Department wants the American Ambassador in
> Tokyo to take this matter up with the Japanese
> Minister of Foreign Affairs.[84]

The next day, Tokyo issued a statement saying it would not interfere with the International settlement where RCA was located. Then Japan sent an ultra-nationalist sect of Buddhist monks to Shanghai's International District to shout anti-Chinese slogans. In response, a Chinese mob killed one monk and injured two others. Heavy fighting broke out, a factory was burned to the ground, and the Japanese killed two Chinese. When the dust settled, China appealed to the League of Nations to help with negotiating a troop withdrawal. I was grateful I wasn't in Shanghai but sensed growing tension in Tokyo.

The uproar was bound to make the papers and catch my mother's attention when she read the morning paper. She worried about me, especially now that I had agreed to stay longer. But, I guess that's what mothers do. Her mothering was one of the reasons I chose to stay, knowing she was keeping an eye on Barbara and Georgie. I trusted her completely. She couldn't seem to accept that I was a capable thirty-five-year-old. Maybe it was because I was her youngest. I made a mental note to write her.

Ma wrote me three days after the Shanghai Incident and once a week thereafter. I found little time to write back. Before I left home, I told her that as long as she didn't get a radiogram, I was okay, and she shouldn't worry. I'd told her, "Ma, RCA will take care of me. This is a great opportunity, and they need me. I know you will keep an eye on Kay and the children and give me the straight scoop. I'll be fine. We'll be fine. Don't fret."

When I couldn't put off a letter any longer, I avoided politics and reassured her that all was well. And now I had to tell her I was headed back to Manchuria—Manchuko—to clean up the mess from the Japanese takeover:

Dear Ma,
I have your letters in front of me unanswered. Time gets the best of me, and a week rolls around like a single day.

Many thanks tho for your nice letters and your kindness to see my children so often. Am very glad to hear they are well and doing nicely.
Just three days ago, I extended myself to live in a quiet place and signed up for a lovely place in Kamakura. A five-room Japanese-style house plenty of sliding glass doors and paper doors etc. Altho furnished foreign-style. Fireplace in each of the two bedrooms, living room, and dining room. Have a "Kimona" to cook and look after the place. Beautiful garden and in another month it will be too wonderful, I think. Also, there is an enclosed summer house up a tiny hill in the yard, and from there, it looks out over the ocean. The house is well protected — lots of trees etc. — and yet the ocean is only about 400 yards away. Figured I

would catch up on some sunburn and swimming…This is about an hour's ride on the fast electric train from my office. How you would enjoy this, Ma—it is so swell that in view of what happened today, I think it must be a dream!

Just three days … and today finds me with a message from New York to proceed to Manchuria at once. So I have to let the place go because I don't know how long I'll be in Mukden and other cities over there! Gee, it is awful because I was never in love with such a place to live before, and I thought maybe you could get up pep enough for another boat ride and enjoy this remarkable spot. Well, maybe later! Will be awful busy the next two or three days — packing up just after unpacking…Maybe gone for three weeks, but it may be three months or six months. Have to get acquainted with the newly organized Mukden government and re-establish our radio-telegraph service between Manchuria and S.F. Will hope I come out of it OK. It is not too easy because there is always plenty of politics and competition in a thousand Chinese ways… Don't worry any because it is quite safe, and the American newspapers all stretch their imagination with big headlines…

Much love, George[85]

I hated leaving our love nest, Japan, and my "Kimona," Nina. As far as I knew, none of my brothers ever kept a woman. I don't think any of them even had an affair. There was a certain status in keeping a mistress, which gave me a sense of confidence I didn't have before. I liked the prestige, and the thrill of keeping a mistress akin to a

Danna. Being an hour from the office, I could tuck Nina away, keep the gossip at bay, maintain an air of respectability, and be free to take out others. It never hurt to be the escort of a wealthy client's daughter. So far, Nina and I had been discrete, staying in separate rooms when we traveled if "Mrs. Street" wouldn't work and eating apart when the Winterbottoms were here. I never even introduced Nina to them. Mrs. Winterbottom was as Victorian as my mother, and I didn't want her disapproval. And I was sick of living out of a suitcase. Coming home to Nina and a home-cooked meal, sitting in front of a fire kept my longing for Georgie and Barbara at bay.

To make matters more regrettable, I received my membership approval for the American Club Tokyo on the first of March. American businessmen established the club hoping to breach the wall between our cultures after the Immigration Act of 1924 barred Japanese and Asians from immigrating to the U.S. The Japanese community regarded the Act as racist and demeaning.

The club was in the top three stories of the Iwamoto Building across the street from the Imperial Hotel, with a view of the palace, a perfect place for wooing potential clients. Winterbottom had encouraged my membership, and RCA paid the bill. I regretted setting aside the opportunity, but New York wanted the Murkden station operational. They pressured the State Department to continue its diplomatic efforts regarding our plant at Chenju. In short order Sheck received permission from the Consul General to repair the power lines and connections damaged during the Shanghai Incident.
86

While Sheck held down the fort in Shanghai, I headed to Mukden. I was reluctant to take Nina. She, of course, was not happy with my decision, but I put my foot down. When I told her, she exploded, "George, NO! You tell RCA go to hell. Don't leave me! I no have job! What I do?"

"I can't afford to keep this place while I'm in Manchuria."

"You stop sending money to Kay. Then you be okay. I stay here."

"Nina, that is not going to work. You know I wish I could, but I will not stop sending money to Kay. She needs it for my children."

"She pay for children not you. Mother take care of children. I take care of you. Who take care of me? Move, move, move, is all we do. What I do? She wailed. "You put me back on street? Evil man!"

She swooned. She pleaded. She cried. She used all her feminine

Safe Conduct pass
(*George Street Archive*)

wiles, and they worked. In the end, I paid three months in advance on our lease in Kamachura so she could stay. And I gave her spending money so I wouldn't have to suffer from guilt. Now I was taking care of two women and two children. It's a good thing I had some savings.

Before entering Manchuria—now called Manchukuo with Henry Puyi as the new emperor of the puppet state—the new government issued a pass that I had to wear around my neck at all times. It was cardboard with a hole punched at the top for a string. On the front, in kana or katakana symbols—I couldn't tell—was my name and permission for safe conduct. On the back in English was "Kwangtung (Manchuria) Army Pass No. 1."

When I arrived at Mukden, I was shocked to see how it had changed. Japanese guards with pointed fleece-lined caps and ear flaps stood guard with fixed bayonets throughout the city. They wrapped their legs from their ankles to the bottom of their knee-length pants. Belted leather vests over thick long-sleeved shirts kept them warm. In my Western attire, I stood out like a sore thumb, and the soldiers were quick to inspect my tag and me.

I was assigned a "traveling companion," a commissioner of the Kwangtung army. I was under constant surveillance as an un-welcome but necessary presence. Other Americans, cloistered at specific clubs and hotels, gave me some sense of security while I walked the tightrope of Chinese and Japanese diplomacy.

My Kwangtung guard "found" a well mounted collection of Japanese postage stamps which he gave to me along with the new issues of Manchukuo[87] when he learned I was a collector.

I was glad I'd left Nina behind. Her heavy accent would have given her away. Besides, there was no way the army would issue such a pass to her. They'd brand her as a spy.

Japan's and China's relations were as tenuous and lethal as a snake hunting a mouse. Just when I figured things would return to normal, on May 15th, The League of Blood and a faction of the Japanese Imperial Navy and Army cadets assassinated the Prime Minister in an attempted military coup d'état. They were determined to wrench political control from the existing government and put it in the hands of the military.

All I wanted was out.

I was pleased to find minor damage done to the equipment at the transmission station in Mukden. Most of it I could repair myself.

After confirming that the operators could run the repaired equipment in Mukden, I headed back to Tokyo and Nina to hunker down with her at the hotel. That evening I took her to the American Club, where I introduced her as Nina—no last name, no Mrs. Street, simply Nina, my little secret, my geisha. She looked good on my arm in her backless silk dress and played her part well.

chapter 16

Struck

1932
Japan

After the tenseness of Manchukuo, I headed to Kobe for a bit of work and pleasure, and I took "Mrs. Street" with me. We stayed a couple of nights at a bathing resort on Suma beach at Osaka Bay on the Inland Sea. The water was crystalline—the air warm, and the views magnificent. I couldn't help but think of Georgie and Barbara, remembering their antics and laughter at Alameda beach. Gazing at the ocean as it gently stacked and rolled over to release its pent-up energy, I was reminded of my children tumbling in the grass.

Nina *(George Street Archive)*

"Nina, I miss Georgie and Barbara. I want to go home soon." We were at the beach's edge. Veils of water wrap around a partially submerged branch like a wind-whipped scarf, and I caught Nina's eye.

"What happen me when you go?" Nina asked as an incoming wave slipped over her feet before hissing away.

The sun winked through the clouds dappling the water's surface with patches of light. "I don't know what will happen. Maybe, I can come back to visit. I will miss you."

"Children, come go. I here forever. You stay. They visit." she said and water splashed our feet. Tears welled in her eyes. We had never talked about parting.

I bent and cupped the ocean in my hand, letting it drip through my fingers, knowing it had kissed the shores of my children's home in California. I had to return with or without Nina.

The water receded. All that was left was a line in the sand.

"I'll figure out something. Let's not get upset, especially today," I said. I turned my face toward the sun's warmth and draped my arm around Nina like a shawl.

I swam twice that day to renew my spirit, fighting the ocean's pull, losing myself in its sound, and letting its strength lift my mood as I gazed over the top of its surface to the edge of nothingness.

That evening, Nina and I sat on the beach enveloped in the warmth of the sand. Darkness overtook the ocean. Pin pricks of lights blinked through the liquid blackness before us becoming indistinguishable from the stars until one swung toward us. The boat's lantern threw a beam in the form of a cross across the darkness. I asked myself, "Had Ma seen the cross of light when I set sail for the first time? Did she stand and stare at the horizon—that line between ocean and sky where the unknown begins and the known disappears? Did she worry about her children knowing they were out of her reach as I do now? What would Ma do if she was in my shoes?"

Turning from my thoughts, I walked arm in arm with Nina back to our room. She cuddled into the crook of my arm as we fell asleep and I listened to the breathing of the ocean. I found myself trying to match its rhythm—exhaling when the sea quieted, inhaling when the waves grabbed the sand. I soon relaxed and fell into sync with the rise and fall of Nina's chest before I slipped into a deep sleep.

***

The next day was overcast, the rollers further from shore. Only the seabirds would swim today.

Nina and I walked the shoreline, careful to sidestep the tendrils of water that tried to pull us into their froth. The surf was wild, stirred by unseen weather. A flock of gulls swirled off the rocks to escape a breaking wave. The ocean did not want two legged animals breaking the patterns of her surface. Green and white water with patches of suspended sand drifted back to the sea reminding me that I was like that patch. Drifting where radio demanded, rising and falling, and breaking around the rocks in my life.

"You like ocean?" Nina asked.

"Yes. It called me when I was eighteen."

"In Russia I watch ships coming, going. I wonder what see. What favorite place you see?"

"Hawaii."

"Why you not stay on ships?"

"I got sick of floating around on a bucket of bolts with a bunch of rough-cut blokes who preferred cards to conversation. They were as baffled by the words I pulled from the ether as I was by their brawn. I tried to explain wireless to a couple of them. Most dropped out of school before I did. At least I made it to the last year of high school."

"Why you stop school?"

"I fell in love with wireless radio."

"I go school until I thirteen, until Reds come and kill Whites. I wonder if little brother alive. Russian Council say forget him, forget parents. I lonesome many times."

"I get lonesome too, missing my children."

We packed when we returned to our room, refreshed and ready for the next phase of our journey. Porters loaded our bags into one of the rickshaws clustered on both sides of the sidewalk. "The Oriental Hotel," the doorman barked.

"I like hotel," Nina said as she gathered her skirt to exit the rickshaw and step onto the large flight of stairs that elevated us above the street's dust. Three arches formed a portico to keep the rain off. "I like Western built. Reminds me little bit of Russia," she said.

A doorman in a crisp white shirt welcomed us into the lofty lobby.

"I'm glad you approve, 'Mrs. Street,'" I said as we signed in as a married couple at the reception deck. "It's a favorite of mine. We'll have Kobe beef for dinner tonight."

"When you come here before?" she asked.

"I came here with Sheck when I first arrived in the Orient. Westerners come in droves when the port opened to foreign trade.

There are jazz clubs, a cinema, and even a cricket club. Sheck and I had a ball."

"Were you bad boy?" she asked.

Of course, I said, "no."

After a couple of days of work, Nina begged for a night at the Rokkosan Hotel. How could I not take her? Twenty-four hundred feet above sea level, the hotel clung to the side of Mt. Rokko like a cliff swallow. The only way to get to the hotel was by a cable car or rope-way, as the locals called it.

"We go this weekend," she cooed as she snuggled her body against mine. What Nina wanted, Nina got—usually. I would get mine later.

We packed an overnight case and headed to the depot on Friday. Nina's excitement was palpable as we made our way to the ropeway. The red cable car resembled an enclosed ski lift. We sat and a slight breeze rocked the lift as we left the platform with a jolt.

"George!" Nina exclaimed. And she grabbed my hand and gripped the wooden bench. "Is safe?"

"Well, it's too late to think about that now. We are on our way."

She buried her head in my shoulder as our angle of ascent steepened. Waist-high windows afforded a stunning view of the mountainside and the valley below.

"Don't close your eyes. It will just make it worse," I told Nina. "Pick a point on the mountainside and stare at it or enjoy the view. Don't be a scaredy-cat."

The rope-way took us to the base of the hotel stairs, and Nina scrambled out, relieved to have her feet on the ground. A red and white striped pole flew the Japanese flag. Pendants stretched to the building, reminding me of a May Pole. Porters took our luggage to our room while we took in the view through the telescopes that lined the porch—Kobe and the ocean spread under our feet like an embroidered carpet.

When darkness descended, the soft glow of the city blended into a limitless pincushion of stars. Then fog blanketed the land and enclosed the sky after the full moon rose and turned off the stars. If my children were here, I would never leave Japan or Nina.

The next day, after our harrowing descent in the cable car made worse by Nina's fear, we return to the Oriental Hotel. I settled Nina in our room and I called on potential clients. That evening, I participated in the bowling tournament at the Kobe Club and dined with several acquaintances. At 11:00 PM walked my friend to his ship bound for Shanghai.[88]

"George, you look drunk," he teased as we shook hands goodbye.

"Maybe, I am. Fun evening but I've got one helluva headache. You have a safe trip and I'll see you next time. I'm going to head back to my hotel."

We parted ways in good cheer, but explosions erupted in my head. When I arrived at my hotel, I stumbled on the stairs and crawled into bed next to Nina. Sleep eluded me as fireworks continued to burst in my brain.

By morning, I was hurting. A volcano of white agony cruised through my body. And I vomited.

Nina wiped my brow with a cold cloth. She'd slept in the chair. "You toss and turn," she said. "You drink much, bad hangover." She frowned and shook her head, then held the trash can to my face when I retched again. "I no want to clean up another mess," she said.

"Nina, I think it's the flu. I've been a heck of a lot drunker, and I've never had a headache like this before." I struggled to my feet, determined to get to the bathroom before I made a bigger mess. While I hugged the toilet, the maid changed our sheets, damp from sweat.

I toughed it out for three days. My stomach settled and the headache lightened. My bowels no longer rebelled, but my limbs cramped. The pain took my breath away. I was sure my muscles were ripping apart, detaching from my bones. A throb flashed up my arm, and I collapsed onto the floor and writhed.

Through my cries, Nina said, "George, you too bad sick. I call cab."

"Take me to Yokohama Hospital," I managed to say.[89] I'd never been this sick in my life. Heck, cutting out my tattoo was easy by comparison. Whatever I had now was beyond me. Nina gave me a sponge bath, shaved my face, and helped me pull on my suit.

We stumbled down the grand staircase as I willed my legs to move. Nina steadied my gait.

We drew disapproving looks from the patrons as we staggered like drunken sailors. "Such behavior in the afternoon!" one old biddy said to no one and everyone.

"Nina, don't say a word. It'll just make matters worse," I managed to say, embarrassed. I could see the fire in her eyes and feared she'd make a scene.

Each step was agony. I could barely move. Sweat dripped from my forehead.

Nina waived a houseboy over and said loud enough for all to hear, "My husband very sick. Please help." And she glared at the woman who had made me blush.

Nina settled me in a cab and then checked us out of the hotel. The cab driver helped me board the train for Yokohama.

The three-hour ride was torture. I remember Nina wiping my brow and recruiting a porter to assist me off the train and into a rickshaw. Each footfall of the puller sent searing bolts of electrical fire through my legs. Fortunately, the hospital was close. The rickshaw driver helped me into the hospital and a chair while Nina searched for an English-speaking doctor.

Minutes stretched into what felt like hours before a doctor strode down the hall with Nina at his heel. "What seems to be the problem?" he asked.

"He very bad sick." Nina said before I could say a word. "You fix."

I did my best to describe my symptoms between Nina's "Very bad, very sick, you fix" demands. The doctor instructed a nurse to help me to an examination room. Nina tromped behind us and followed us. The nurse insisted she leave.

"Nina, please," I said when she made a fuss. "Wait."

The doctor poked and prodded and diagnosed me with ptomaine poisoning. Food poisoning.

I'd had it before. Not this bad. But I'd beat it then, and I'd beat it again. I drank a ton of water, didn't eat, and my stomach settled, but my limbs continued to cramp horribly. The doctor gave me morphine.

I drifted out of my world of pain and into a kaleidoscope of sights and sounds. Light and time swirled, and my life flickered like a disjointed silent film. After five long days of endless cycles of pain and morphine, I could no longer feel my legs. Nina never left my side as far as I could tell.

During a lucid moment, Nina said, "George, doctors no good. You not getting better. They keeping you drugged up. Hope for the best."

"You're right," I managed. "Arrange for an ambulance to get me to St. Luke's in Tokyo." If they can't help me, nobody can."[90]

I spoke to the doctor and discharged myself. Nina and a nurse helped me dress before attendants lifted me onto the gurney. Wheels clacked, and overhead, lights blurred as they whisked me to the waiting ambulance.

At St. Luke's, I was poked and prodded again. Nina's rantings barely penetrated my subconscious. Pain overcame me, and I longed for the relief of morphine. Finally, the nurse gave me a shot, and a fog washed over me.

When I surfaced, the doctor said, " I'm sorry to have to tell you this but you have poliomyelitis. Polio. Infantile paralysis.

I laid in stunned silence. Nina gasped. Time stopped. And the air was sucked out of the room.

chapter 17

Shattered

1932
Japan

"Polio??" I cried. "How could I have polio? Children get polio! You can't be right!" I was as angry as I'd ever been. I would have thrown my bedpan if I could, but my arms were as stiff as my legs.

"I'm sorry," the doctor said.

"Sorry? Is that all you can say? I've got food poisoning. What kind of doctor are you? Get me some who knows what they are doing. You can't be right." My heart quickened and I could barely breathe.

Overlooking my rudeness the doctor replied, "We have a Japanese doctor who specializes in polio cases. He is excellent. I will get him and a translator."[91]

After much back and forth, the new doctor confirmed the diagnosis. He told me polio was a virus transmittable to anyone regardless of age. All my symptoms and suffering were consistent with the disease. The translator said, "He is very sorry."

I gaped at the English-speaking doctor and asked, "How could I have gotten this? I've been careful about drinking boiled water and have only eaten at the best restaurants."

"All it takes is one person to transmit it—a waiter, a rickshaw driver, a server."

He continued, "I'm sorry. There is no cure. You could get better, or you could get worse. It would be best if you went back to the United States. We will help you get to a point where you can travel. I will do my best for you."

The doctors left with those words hanging like spider webs from the ceiling. The ones that kept looping through my brain were: "There is no cure."

Nina sat like a stone in the bedside chair. There was no warmth in her eyes, just cold-hard reality reflecting back at me like the stark tile walls of my new prison.

Panic rose like bile. "Don't leave me Nina," I said and I beat on my legs with my good arm.

Polio. How could I have polio? Good God, what was I to do? I couldn't even write a letter to Ma. I couldn't work. I was in a foreign country, relying on a foreign doctor. How was I going to pay for all this? I was a useless slab of meat with a head full of worry. What *was* I going to do if I didn't get better? The doctor's had to be wrong.

When denial gave way to the truth, I reached out to the kind gentleman who had provided me desk space when I first arrived in

Tokyo. Ushizawa was seventy-two and the Councilor of Japan Wireless Telegraph. On June 21st, I dictated a letter to him. A nurse wrote the words I couldn't. When she read what I'd said, we polished my distress onto stationary, making light of my situation, not wanting to create hardship for others. Besides, saying more wouldn't change the facts.

```
Mr. Ushizawa
R.C.A. Communications
Jiji Building,
Tokyo

My dear Mr. Ushizawa:
Mr. Street requests that you send the following
letter to Mr. Winterbottom.

"This is to inform you that I had gone to Kobe
for three weeks work when, June 11, I became
ill. At the time, I thought it was probably
influenza, but having made no recovery after
three days, I returned home, and on June 14,
entered the Yokohama General Hospital, where I
was told I had ptomaine poisoning. Finding the
service there inadequate, I moved by ambulance
to Tokyo on June 19 and entered St. Luke's
Hospital, where I am at present, confined for
treatment    of    poliomyelitis    (Infantile
Paralysis). At present, both legs and one arm
are completely useless, and they cannot say what
the progress of the disease will be. You will
have later information by letter or radiogram.

Very sincerely yours,
George Street
```

Mr. Street would, of course, like to have this
letter sent immediately. Naturally, he prefers
to have as little as possible said about his
condition among his Tokyo associates at the
present time. Within a few days or a week, we
may be able to give more definite information
about him.
Sincerely yours,
H. K. Shipps (for George Street)[92]

Next, I dictated a similar letter to Ma but added words of
encouragement because she'd be frantic:

...I am hoping that they [legs and arm] may
recover when the acute stage of the disease has
passed. I know how you will think about this
and I shall endeavor to think and pray the same
way. I am unable to write myself, and this
letter is being written through the kindness of
a member of the hospital staff.

I shall let you know more in a short time. If
anything more serious occurs, we shall send you
a radiogram so that if you have not heard by
radiogram at the time this letter arrives, you
may be sure that I am getting better rather than
worse.
Lovingly,
George[93]

I also asked the nurse to send my mother a separate letter of
reassurance. She wrote: "This is just a note to assure you that every
possible care is being given to your son, who is in a private room
with day and night special nurses...Mr. Street is under the care of
two physicians, one an excellent Japanese physician trained in

America, and the other a well-trained American doctor. His condition is serious, but I want you to know that all is being done that is medically possible."[94]

My letter would crush Ma. She'd rally the family and gather my children to her breast. Clarence would probably tell Kay. I dictated another letter to Ma three days later:

> Dear Ma,
> Here is another letter thru the kindness of one of the St Luke's hospital staff. I just want to let you know that I have received two letters from you within the last few days telling me that Betty Fehldman is returning to Honolulu. I can imagine that it will make you very lonely at first not to have her. Thank you very much for your kindness in giving Barbara a birthday party. I am glad to know that both of my children are doing well and have received good marks in school...I have now been flat on my back for fourteen days, and it is very hard as I have great pain and cramps in my legs, back, and one arm. In another three weeks or so, I should have regained my strength, so I'll just stick it out as best I can in the meantime. I do not wish to alarm you, but I am indeed in poor physical condition. How this illness came about is still a mystery to me as I have taken more than ordinary care of myself since coming out here...
>
> With love and affection,
> George[95]

It was the pull of people who cared that propelled me forward, the hope of recovery that kept me fighting. By July 9th—a month after I'd been shattered by this horrible disease—I sent a letter to Winterbottom to let him know that I had not suffered much pain over the last week and regained considerable strength in my right leg and arm. Massage and electrical treatments helped, thanks to the morphine injections they gave me before each session. I told him within two or three weeks, I might walk! I wanted to reassure him that I'd soon be back on the job. In my enthusiasm, I dictated:

```
I understand that Mr. Shecklen thought that it
would be necessary that I return to the United
States in order to fully recover. That was also
the idea of the number one doctor in charge of
my case, but it seems now that the actual
attendants who are working on me do not think
this at all necessary…Japan Wireless has been
very kind, as have many friends and
acquaintances made during the past months. I
hope by the time this letter reaches you, I
shall be able to send a service[gram] saying I
am quite O.K.

Again thanking you,
Very sincerely yours,
George Street[96]
```

RCA paid for my care which was a huge relief.[97] I only needed to use my savings for Nina's living expenses. She stayed in the Kamakura house, hopping the train to be at my side. I was grateful she stayed, but, true to form she continued to drive the staff crazy with her demands.

George in a wheelchair at Yokohama General Hospital
(George Street Archive)

By the end of July, an acquaintance and reporter for the Shimsun Rengo news agency came by to convey the well-wishes of the general foreign correspondent for RCA, confirming my fear that letters and radiograms were circulating about my condition. What would people think? What assurances could I give my clients? How would they react to a cripple if I didn't get better? And Ma? What would she think?

Winterbottom wrote on the eighth of August with promises that I could remain at my job in Tokyo indefinitely. He hinted at his disappointment about us not sending facsimile pictures of the Olympics games. I could have accomplished it if I'd been at work. What must he think? I agonized over my prospects.

On that same day, I also received a letter from the Manager of the Commercial Department of RCA. He'd overheard Winterbottom say I would remain in Tokyo because they had no replacement. Besides, he'd indicated my solicitation work in Japan paid off.

By the twenty-second of August, I could hold a pen! I was like I'd conquered Mt. Everest and lived to tell the tale. I could sit upright in a chair, and although my penmanship wasn't the best, it was legible. I immediately hand wrote a letter to Ma. I had received a letter from Georgie, and I was pleased with his improved handwriting. Mine was almost as good. I wrote:

Dear Ma,

Thank you also for the trouble of having him at your house for a week. Thank you for the information about Kathryn. Beginning this year, I have only sent what I must and nothing extra. I put quite a bit into insurance, so I cut out all additional donations, and besides it is best, as you say, because she uses it mostly on herself. So far, she has never asked me for any extra money, now four years, but also, she hardly ever thanks me when I send from $10 to $25 extra per month. Anytime she cannot or does not want to keep the children, I hope to still have the means to do it myself.[98]

Ma's watchful eye hovering over my children eased my mind. Nina and morphine kept me going. I imagined that the hopeful words I'd been writing would come true. After all, I was improving. I could hold a pen!

chapter 18

Stuck

1932
Japan

Mr. Street, telegram," a nurse said as she walked over to my bed to hand it to me. I was in my usual position—my upper body supported by pillows, my useless legs stretched out in front of me and tucked neatly under a bedsheet. I grasped the letter with my left hand. My right was acting up.

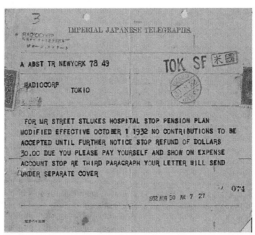

Radiogram from RCA *(George Street Archive)*

The radiogram said I no longer had to pay into my pension plan. Thank goodness. Not working was taking a toll on my wallet. I'd received hundreds of letters and cards from well-wishers, but none contained money—not that I wanted charity.

According to Ma, my wealthy Tante Marie wanted me to write. She is a grand old lady who addresses her prayers to God but takes all the credit for herself. I asked Ma, "What can I write to her? It seems to me that she always looks to herself first. I once asked her for assistance which she could have easily afforded but never received a dime."[99]

Then Ma and my sister-in-law, Janice, wanted to come over. What would I do with them? I can't show them around, and I'm not interested in people staring at me and feeling sorry for me. They could stay at my Kamakura house, but then I'd have to explain Nina. I could not afford to pay additional hotel bills while doling out money for the never-ending assistance that didn't qualify as a hospital bill.

I politely declined Ma's offer and asked her to keep an eye on my children since she mentioned Kay again in her latest letter. I had told Kay dozens of times that I was ready and capable of looking after them and making a good home for them, barring my present condition, of course. Kay's constant whining about money had driven me crazy when we lived together; it drove me crazier now. She wrote that she'd gone to a fortune-teller and she told her something terrible would happen to me. Well, it did. The fortune teller was right. I reassured Kay that I'd continue sending support payments for the children. I wasn't dead yet.

Nina said for the hundredth time while she sat beside me during my morphine treatment, "George, you addicted. You be like bums in

Little Russia if no stop. Sleeping in dirt, peeing in pants. What I do when you passed out? Whore for money?"

"Nina, stop." I was sick of women clucking and pecking at me like *Henny Penny and The Sky is Falling.* "Maybe you should try the electric treatments and see how long you'd last without morphine. I need it to dull the pain. I'm doing the best I can to get out of here. I've got feeling in my right hand and arm most days. I can type now. If my legs would only sit–up and take notice, we'd be out of here."

Always one to have the last word, Nina said, "Morphine not good," she said to the attendant as he gave me a shot.

As soon as the plunger hit bottom, my world swirled into a welcoming fog, free of pain. My muscles relaxed. My mind emptied. Even Nina disappeared—for a while. I imagined it like death. Nothingness. No awareness of my body, no connection to my mind, no sense of time or place. Nothingness.

I slowly emerged when my brain was done with its morphine bath. Lights and crenulated arches, grids, ladders, and dots swirled behind my eyelids. I struggled to organize the images and noises. After a while, patterns turned recognizable, words made sense, and I was back feeling like I had arisen from the dead into the clutter and chaos of reality. As soon as I returned, I longed for the relief, the freedom, and the nothingness.

Days slipped into weeks, and my legs did not improve. I wrote to Ma: "If I stayed here a hundred years, I would probably recover on my own accord, but a long time at 35 yen per day is a lot of money. I heard of a German doctor in Yokohama thru friends. He has treated this affliction before, and altho he is very expensive, I decided to move to Yokohama to come under his care."[100]

Nina was on board. "I be nurse. Save many yen. You pay hotel, food, and doctor."

Her willingness to care for me cinched my heart. She learned how to transfer me to a chair and change the bedsheets by rolling me from one side to the other. Since she'd seen and loved every part of me, she had no jitters when bathing and shaving me, unlike a couple of the younger nurses. She'd repeatedly said, "Taking care you better than Little Russia."

I took her at her word, grateful she was willing to deal with my useless body.

On 24 August, I received my discharge letter from Dr. H. Hashimoto

Nina said. "I get ambulance. You take a little bit of morphine. We go to Hotel New Grand. Much better place than hospital."

"I hope you're right," I said and tried not to think about my dependence upon my mistress in a place where I couldn't speak the language while battling a disease with no cure. The very thought sent waves of panic through my body. Thank god for morphine!

Nina picked the New Grand because it could accommodate my wheelchair—two elevators, wide hallways, and spacious lounge rooms. She arranged for a wingback chair and a floor lamp by our door so an attendant could wait comfortably. She also had an extra wardrobe moved to our room.

A porter helped me from the ambulance to my chair when we arrived. Nina took over from there and wheeled to the front desk.

The receptionist brought the ledger to me to sign, leaving her station and walking around the polished reception desk. I checked us in as Mr. and Mrs. Street. It was too fine a hotel for the truth.

"Thank you, I said. "I guess I'll have to get used to this—strangers helping me and having to look up to see a face."

It was depressing. I was once lanky and proud. Now, I sat no higher than a child. The registrar smiled and held the book so I could write our names. At least I could hold a pen.

By the time we wheeled to our room, I was exhausted. The porter filled the dresser drawers, hung my suits and Nina's dresses, and placed my typewriter on the desk.

I hugged Nina when he left, pressing my face into her waist. "How can I not get better in such a place?" My mental anguish was as acute as the pain. I loved my job and had accomplished much in the previous year and a half. How could I possibly complete this assignment when I was flat on my back? Would RCA retain me? How would I manage to live? Would I end up singing the Great Depression refrain like so many others?

> America is the land of the free,
> Free without a doubt,
> For if you have no food to eat,
> You're free to go without.[101]

I said to Nina. "I cannot expect the company to continue to pay my bills forever. But I am not worrying one way or the other because worry won't build new muscles and strength. You picked a fine place for us. Thank you."[102]

The next day, Nina took me to a bathhouse to help me relax. I wasn't ready for the Roman-style bath where men and women soaked together nude, so I requested a separate room. Nina left and went shopping. Bumbling in butchered Japanese, I chose a male attendant, my Victorian upbringing surfacing once again.

My attendant helped me remove my clothes and hung them in an adjoining private ante-room. He sent my shoes out for a shine and turned on the water in the tiled tub. The front half was about twice as deep as the back, like a chair. He eased me onto a low stool and threw a bucket of water on me. My upper body bolted upright, shocked by the cold. He then proceeded to soap me down—but good—and lowered me into the tile tub. After a good long soak, he reappeared to help me dress. All this cost thirty-five cents. It was one of the most relaxing indulgences I'd ever experienced.[103]

I think it was here that I fell in love with Japan and its discreet people who shined with the brilliance of a culture that stretched into the past. They have a quiet fierceness and keep their judgments to themselves, never questioning Nina's posing as my wife, tolerating my crass Western ways. I had been a head taller than most, but no longer. I admired them as they graciously helped me navigate even the simplest pleasures.

When I returned to the hotel, I sat at the window, as relaxed as a bowl of jelly, and wrote to Ma.

"My room overlooks Yokohama harbor, and I can see the ships come and go. Sunday, there was a yacht race, and the finish line was just across the street, which is the edge of the water. If I do not recover more of my former facilities within a month, I imagine I shall be traveling on one of the outgoing steamers. I pray to recover…in order to again actively engage in business. If I come home, what then?"[104]

The following day, Dr. Hermann Grauert, the expert I hoped would get me back on my feet, came to the hotel. He performed a complete examination and prescribed a treatment plan. I continued on morphine to tolerate the pain while he manipulated and massaged my limbs. Wool compresses soaked in hot water relaxed my leg muscles.[105] To this day, the smell of wet wool sickens me. He then locked my legs in braces to prevent them from deforming when they convulsed. His words rang in my ears, "Hard work and determination are your biggest allies." I had both, but would they be enough?

Asian maids, dressed in Swiss outfits, cleaned the room. I could tell they feared getting polio while they were around me. They bowed, bent low, and kept their distance. People in the lounge coyly moved away. Waiters brought our meals to the room. Friends stood at a distance, shook their heads, and talked in platitudes:

"George, you old brick, you'll be up and about in no time. Keep your chin up. Hard work will do the trick," they'd say. Over time, I wanted no part of their cheery banalities. I was a cripple, as stiff as the old brick they called me.

My days consisted of eating, dressing—a significant effort even with Nina's help—Dr. Grauert's visits, and resting. I was strong enough to wheel my chair to a spot in the sun so I could read the paper or not. There I sat like a cat gazing out the window at other people's lives. I willed my mind to empty as I tried to face the horror of my new world. Wondering why, thinking back. Remembering what it was like to walk, to climb, to run. I recalled the stroll Nina, and I took to the Hirano-Jinja shrine when we were in Kyoto. We marveled at the ancient cherry trees planted in the eighth century. Clouds of pink and white petals fell to our feet like snowflakes in a winter storm. The scent of almonds and honey rose to greet us with each footfall. How I longed to walk among the cherry trees again. I chuckled, remembering Nina's elbow in my side when I stared at a geisha as she floated by on lacquered zori, mincing her steps and nodding in silence when she caught my eye.

Would I ever be able to step aside for a geisha again or stroll in a market packed with vendors? Only time will tell.

Dr. Grauert said he could help me. I sure hope he is right. I could not walk or stand, but the cramping and seizures had diminished. With his encouragement, I could assist Nina with transferring my useless body from the bed to the wheelchair. She still had to swing my legs, but I could bear more weight on my arms, making it easier for her. He came every day, and he helped me a lot.

I learned from a colleague that the Mukden station was running satisfactorily under the new Manchukuo regime. I welcomed the distraction of business concerns. Manchukuo continued to insist on a new contract with RCA, and RCA continued to resist. The Far Eastern Affairs division chief wanted to know when a representative from RCA—me—would confer with the new Manchukuo government. As much as I wanted to, it was impossible. How would I get there? Where could I stay? Would they trust a cripple in a wheelchair? I was stuck—trapped in a useless body, dependent on others, at the mercy of morphine—stuck.

RCA waited as long as they could to replace me. They had a business to run and couldn't wait for me forever. They had to cut me loose. My brain understood, but my heart didn't. After all my years in their employ, couldn't they have hung on a little longer? What was I supposed to do? How would I support myself? Would I rot in the Orient? At least RCA had to pay for my passage back to the States. That was something.

I had to head home while I still had money—if I could.

chapter 19

"Dear Ma"

1932
Japan

At the end of August, when it became apparent that I had to return to the States, I began the process of finding a way home.

"George, I come with you," Nina said. "Help you on ship. I get visa to United States. I take care of you."

"Nina, don't box me in a corner. I can't think myself out of a wet paper bag right now. Do you even have your birth certificate?"

She rummaged among her papers and found it. It was in Russian. "Okay, I said, "If you can get a visa, I'll pay you to help me when we are on the ship. That way, you'll have some money once we get to San Francisco. I will be at Dante's Sanatorium, so I don't know what I can do for you once we arrive."

"I get job. Real job. I help," Nina said.

Who knows what she would find with her limited English?

"I survivor," she said.

"That you are. We both are," I said. "Okay, let's get you a visa," and we set our sails for foggy seas. Who knows what was on the other side? We'd find out when we got there.

I paid for a translation of her birth certificate and consulted with an attorney about what documentation Nina would need. First, Nina had to get letters affirming she wasn't a criminal and was of good moral character. She obtained a letter from the Shanghai commissioner of police stating her record was clear. The Council of the United Russian Public Organization of Shanghai also issued her a letter. Then she proceeded to get letters of recommendation that attested to her high moral character and diligence. Mrs. A. E. Zaeff, Nina's house mother at her boarding house on Bubbling Well Road in Shanghai wrote, "Nina had been under my personal observation for the past eighteen months living at my home, and I have acted as a chaperon toward her. I can safely state that she is an honest, industrious, and virtuous young lady."[106] She sent the letter directly to the American Consul General.

The landlord of the Kamakura house also sent a letter to the Consul General stating Nina had lived there the last seven months, contradicting Mrs. Zeff's letter. When the consulate asked for an explanation, Nina had Mrs. Zaeff send another letter to correct her first statement. She wrote she had *known* Nina for the past eighteen months and had not lived with her. But it was too late. The falsehood about her residency and having a high moral standard was apparent.

The Consulate denied Nina's visa request. She was devastated, and so was I. What was I going to do? I had to have someone assist me aboard the ship. Nina railed, "George, I stuck here forever. It your fault. You took me away. I good person. Help you much. What I do now?"

"Nina, truth has a way of catching up with you. You have been traveling with me

Recommendation (George Street Archive, Nina Binder 1)

all over China and Japan posing as Mrs. Street—not a virtuous situation by any stretch of the imagination." I said unkindly. "You didn't object at the time. In fact, your 'eagerness' kept me awake many nights."

"You like. You no say no. You make me whore."

"Go away." I finally said. "Go for a walk or something. Let me think."

I considered my alternatives. There was no way I could manage on a ship in a wheelchair without help. I can hire a nurse to accompany me, which would cost a fortune. I could send for Ma, but she wasn't very strong. How could she lift me and pull me up- stairs? One of my brothers or sisters? Ha! My ego wouldn't allow it. At some level, I understood that only Nina could help me survive in this world of strangers, nausea, and constant itching brought on by the opiate I depended upon. At times, I could not breathe, or so it seemed, as my chest heaved. At other times, a thousand points of irritation assaulted my skin. The demonic monster morphine now possessed my body instead of pain. Would *I* ever be able to take back my life?

When Nina returned, her eyes were dull with sadness. Mine too.

"George, what we do?" she asked as she snuggled up to me in my chair.

"I don't know. I'll call my attorney and see what he suggests."

The result of my call: I had to marry her. It was the only way I could bring her to the States since she'd been denied a visa. When I cradled the phone, silence filled the room. It was apparent my future was intertwined with my mistress from Little Russia, this woman who once controlled my manhood with a mere look.

I twisted in my chair to catch her eye. "The attorney said you'd be guaranteed a United States passport if you were my wife." I didn't tell her he also said I could divorce her if it didn't work out. I gave her a long look and said, "Nina, will you marry me?"

She didn't respond right away but instead turned away for a second. Did I see a smile on her face? Was this her ultimate goal all along? Her sister had escaped through marriage. Why shouldn't she?

Her hesitation was brief. She embraced me and said, "Yes, yes, yes. I marry you. I take good care of you. I be best wife."

Fortunately, it was easy to tie the knot in Japan. There was no residency requirement. I had to deliver a written marriage request to the Registrar in Japanese signed by both of us and two witnesses, pay a small fee, and the deed was done. We'd picked out a simple ring. I couldn't afford more.

As it worked out, on September 1st —Kay's birthday—Nina and I were officially married. Nothing fancy. No celebration. Just paperwork and a pronouncement, "You are now man and wife." Nina applied for a passport immediately.

And we waited. While Nina scouted for a ship that could accommodate my wheelchair, I blew through my savings and began to draw down my pension.

In October, Nina received her passport. I had written to the American Consulate attesting that I would be responsible for her maintenance and guaranteed she would not become a public liability. That did the trick. With a passport, Nina could accompany me. Now all we needed was a way to get to the states.

We cloistered at the New Grand while Nina hunted for a ship, and I continued my treatments. With Nina's help, I exercised when the good doctor was unavailable. I wrote to Ma:

Dear Ma,

Well, now, wonder what you will think of this? I am married. I said nothing of it before because I wanted to be sure to be able to get an American visa for my wife, who is of European parentage. Altho my affliction has been a poor honeymoon, she has indeed been a godsend to me and a very great help and comfort. When I moved to this hotel, I did away with the two nurses I had, and this brave girl takes care of me in a most excellent manner. Her papers are now in order, and where I go, she can go…Do not be too much surprised over this because I feel everything eventually regarding my health will be OK…[107]

No ships. We dined at the hotel restaurant on Thanksgiving Day.

On December 1ˢᵗ, Mr. J. F. Harris, my replacement, arrived.

I held a luncheon at the hotel so I could introduce him to the representatives of the Victor Company, Mr. Hashimoto of JWT, and the officials of Teishinsho. It was exhausting, and I left depressed. I reported to Winterbottom on the thirteenth.

> So far Mr. Harris has given me only one opportunity for having a business session with him; a couple of hours one day last week. All files and office correspondence have been turned over to him, and I shall be pleased to assist in any matters not clear whenever he calls before I leave. Concerning myself, I continue to make slow but favorable progress. Cannot stand up yet, but am able to move my body very considerably more than a month ago.
>
> Sincerely, George." [108]

There was no denying it. As much as I had wanted to complete my mission, I was done—headed for home as a cripple with my mistress as my wife. Nina got a real passport, and I got a helpmate. Fair trade? Who knows?

Before Christmas, Nina took the train downtown to try to find me crutches. I could stand for about thirty seconds with my legs braced against the side of the bed before I crumpled. We reasoned that with crutches, I might be able to move about a ship without a chair. If our plan worked, any ship bound for the States would work.

I wrote to Ma.

> "I'll have to teach my legs all over again. The bad left leg is improving all the time, but I

rather doubt that it will ever be normal…I was out in the wheelchair yesterday. Across the street in the Park, which is on the waterfront. Cold wind blowing so only stayed out half an hour."[109]

Nina had returned with crutches, but I was too weak, and my legs noodled into puddles after just a few seconds, no matter how long we practiced. It could take weeks, months, maybe years to build up the endurance needed to work them.

Friends took me for my first automobile ride since I had contracted polio. It wasn't too difficult to get me in and quite easy to get me out. We drove all around Tokyo. Sunday, they took me to the mountains and the famous resort at Miyanoshita. It was a fifty-mile drive each way. I was out for six and a half hours, and it did not tire me even with the bad roads. I stayed in the car while the others had tea inside the Fujiya Hotel. I drank mine in the automobile.

My doctor wanted me to spend a couple of days at the resort to use the mineral water swimming tanks, but we abandoned the plan when we studied the logistics of moving around in a wheelchair.[110] It did me good to get out; it rose my spirits even though we couldn't stay.

Hopeful, I forwarded my mail to Ma's house, hoping that soon I'd be able to collect it, and I took up stamp collecting. It helped pass the time and didn't require any physical activity. Several children and a couple of men swapped stamps with me.

I wrote to Ma on December 22nd to give her a progress report:

Have been trying to strike a bargain with the different steamship lines and now have two good bargains. The first is a freighter that has very nice accommodations for a dozen passengers. Nina will look at the rooms next week, and if it is OK, we shall leave here on that vessel. It is a Norwegian ship *Tai Ying*, and Dodwell & Co. are the S.F. agents. It is due in S.F. January 10th. But I'll radio, and if you do not have a radiogram from me, I'll not be aboard but will come later on some other vessel.

I had a most delightful dream last night. I seldom dream. This is the second dream in which I have gotten up enough strength and put on a pair of shoes, and walked. Oh boy![111]

On Christmas, the hotel held a dinner and dance. We were well known by now, and they invited us as their private guests since no one had gotten polio from me. Nina bought a new outfit. And she dressed me up like a manikin. "George, you so handsome," she said as she adjusted my tie and planted a kiss on my cheek. I smiled, feeling like a puppet on display.

There were about five hundred people in attendance, primarily Japanese. A porter pushed me to the ballroom past the big tree in the lobby and left me at a table while Nina danced. All I could do was watch. She came over to me at one point and took my hands while she moved in front of me.

"George, see we dancing," she giggled, and I became acutely aware of my condition and limitations.

"Nina, I'm tired," I lied. "Please take me back to our room. You can return if you want." We waved, and she wheeled me to an elevator. When she settled me in, she lit the candles on the small tree in our room. Our first Christmas as husband and wife. I couldn't help but wonder what the children were doing. I'd sent presents from Santa.

In my last letter to Ma, I wrote,

```
Unfortunately, when Nina inspected the rooms on
the Tai Yang, the only favorable cabin had
already been booked. It would be another three
to six weeks before we can find another. I am
disappointed because we both are tired of the
hotel. The weather has turned sharp and cold,
so I can't go outside. Nina located some
crutches, but I am not strong enough to hold
myself up on them. The doctor will be away for
a few days, and he wants to see how I do without
injections. Well, I've had enough needles stuck
into my hide. More than 320 of them to date. As
difficult as it will be, I'll tough it out.[112]
```

Nina handwrote a note at the bottom. Her English had improved. Teaching her was the one thing I could do in return for all her help. She wrote: "Hello, mother. Hope you are well. Love and kisses, Nina."[113] What would Ma think about her? What would Georgie and Barbara think about their "new" mother? What would they think of me? All these unknowns. There was only one way to find out. I had to get home.

Nina finally located a ship that could accommodate my chair, and we set sail for San Francisco aboard *SS President Coolidge* on 10 January 1933. RCA footed most of the bill. Winterbottom wouldn't have it any other way. No freighter for us. It was a top-notch luxury liner launched in September. She was huge, the largest merchant ship in the U.S. She accommodated almost a thousand passengers, and the interior trappings were on par with the best hotels. It boasted two saltwater pools which I thoroughly enjoyed, a cinema, and a beauty parlor, which Nina enjoyed, and was air-conditioned throughout. Our cabin had an ensuite bathroom and was first class all the way. At last, I was headed for American soil, American doctors, and my family. It brightened my spirits to know RCA cared enough to ship me home in something other than a box.

chapter 20

"The children will be fine."

1933
SF Bay Area

During our crossing, we had a one-day stopover in Honolulu. Nina and a porter wheeled me down the gangplank to a cab.

After I was settled, Nina said, "George, I never see Honolulu. We go look."

How could I resist? She'd tended me during the eight days it took us to get from Yokohama to Hawaii and she deserved a break. And I deserved one, too.

"Cabby, would you give us a driving tour of Honolulu?" I asked, glad to be back in paradise, happy to be able to speak and listen to English, grateful to be on American soil again.

The cabby drove us past The Royal Hawaiian Hotel, Chinatown, around Diamond Head, to the blow hole, and over the Pali. Nina plastered her face to the window like a schoolgirl eyeing toys at a department store. Memories came crashing back.

c. 1916 Diamond Head in background *(George Street Archive)*

I told Nina, "When I was here in 1916, Waikiki beach was empty except for surfers and a couple of Hawaiians in dugout canoes. The men wore loincloths like the Japanese fisherman on the beach in Kamakura. Cabbie, drive us to Koko Head," I said, "I want to see where I worked in 1920."

"You here long time ago, before I leave Russia," said Nina. "Left. Left Russia, Nina," I corrected and continued. "I bunked at the hotel for radio operators for about two years. I got a Chambers automobile but switched to a Harley-Davidson motorcycle because of the roads. My buddy rode tandem on the bike. The roads and bridges out Koko

Broken Bridge *(George Street Archive)*

Head way were really something. We had to repair the bridges ourselves in order to get to work.

If I took the roadster in heavy rains, I'd get stuck in the mud and have to wait two or three days to dig out."

"What you do then?"

"I carried a sleeping bag and mosquito netting just in case. Usually, in bad road conditions, the Harley got us through."[114]

"You have girlfriend you take on motorbike?" The ever-jealous Nina asked.

"I went on picnics to Hanauma Bay with my buddies and a couple of girls. When we get to San Francisco I'll show you a picture of me wearing a girl's dress over my bathing suit. It was all very innocent."

I didn't tell her about our drunken time when we fashioned hula skirts out of seaweed to entertain the gals. I'd never have heard the end of it.

George (middle) in seaweed hula skirt.
(George Street Archive)

We re-boarded the ship that evening for the five-day crossing to the States. When we arrived in San Francisco, Ma and my brother Henry met us at the pier. Ma presented Nina with flowers. After hugs all around, I could see concern wash over Ma's eyes. I'd lost weight, was a cripple, and needed a shot of morphine. While driving to Ma's house on Bates Street, Nina kept the conversation moving by asking about the sights.

"George, your children are at the house," Ma interjected. "Kay agreed to let them stay for a couple of days so they could visit with you."

"Ma, thanks so much. It's been over two years. I bet they've changed." How would they react to seeing me in a wheelchair? What about Nina? How would they like to have a stepmother?

"Ma, do they know about my polio and Nina?"

"Yes, yes. I told them you'd be in a wheelchair and had a new wife. I explained what that meant. That they had two mothers. I didn't mention her youth. They wouldn't understand the age difference anyway," she said, her voice dripping with disdain.

I hadn't considered that age-wise, Nina was young enough to be my children's older sister. I could tell by Ma's tone of voice that she did not approve. Ma was so old-fashioned. She hadn't liked Kay because of her free spirit. Now she didn't like Nina because of her age. Would Ma ever approve of my choice of women? I squeezed Nina's hand to give her courage. Nina, for once, kept her mouth shut.

"Ma, Nina has been such a godsend. I wouldn't be here without her," I said, and I resumed my monologue, pointing out the sites as we drove.

When we arrived at the house, Barbara and Georgie tumbled down the stairs. Barbara had her arms around me before I could get out of the car. Georgie stood back and then stepped forward to steady my chair while I swung into it. Ma had tears in her eyes.

"Me and children bring in luggage," Nina said, cradling the flowers Ma had given her. Barbara grabbed a case, one small enough for her to manage. George and Henry pulled me up the stairs, one bump at a time. We settled into the living room.

Ma's chair sat by the fireplace, just like before. So much had changed, yet so much was the same. I'd lived a lifetime since my last visit. Nina popped open a suitcase and passed me presents to hand out. She gave Ma embroidered cloth.

"Mother, this for you," Nina said, forgetting her verb again. "I pick myself."

"Thank you, Nina. It's lovely. Whatever shall I do with it?"

"You make dress."

"Oh, it's too bright for me," and Ma set it aside without a second glance.

"I go put flowers in vase," Nina said as she left the room, hurt by Ma's rejection. Nina had fussed over her choice for hours, returning to the shop more than once to make her selection.

I piped up, "Ma, maybe you could make throw pillows out of it. Nina took a lot of time selecting it. It's very fine silk."

"Yes, maybe. I'll speak to Reta about it. She has good taste when it comes to such matters." Dismissed, I focused my attention elsewhere and tried to bury Ma's rudeness.

My children stood before me, My children. My beautiful bright children. Good looking. Healthy. My heart lightened at the sight of them. I held their hand while they answered my questions about school. They hadn't recoiled at the sight of me. Barbara watched her feet, being careful of the front wheels. She did her best to behave, only to speak when spoken to as she had been taught, and to look me in the eye when she spoke.

Nina kept busy, helping the children with their presents and taking the luggage upstairs. Ma and Anna prepared my welcome-home dinner, leaving us men to talk over cigars. My brother Ed joined us, as did Anna's husband. Never one to beat around the bush, Ed confronted the elephant in the room.

"George," he asked, "how will you manage? You can't even get up the stairs to your bedroom." Ever since Dad died in 1920, he had taken on the role of head of household.

I puffed on my cigar. Heady lightness made me snap. "Ed, I'll be fine. I will be here just a couple of days. I plan to become an outpatient at the Dante Sanatorium in the City and get us an apartment. You needn't worry." I resented his asking. I'd gotten myself from Japan to the States. How dare he think I couldn't manage now!

Ed didn't let up. "That's some young thing you've brought home. She can't even speak English."

"That young thing has seen more, done more, and helped me more than you ever have in all the years we've been brothers. I'd appreciate you keeping your thoughts to yourself if you can't be kind."

Ma broke the tension with a call to dinner. Nina sat at my right, Barbara on my left. Georgie was across from me. Ma had set the table with her best china. Candles blazed next to Nina's flowers. It was perfect. Home. Perfect, except for Ed's big mouth.

After dinner, Nina and Georgie pulled me up the stairs to our bedroom. Anna and her husband occupied the other spare bedroom. All the children—Anna had two—camped in the living room. Their giggles lulled me to sleep.

The next day, I made arrangements to enter Dante's. I spent as much time as possible with Georgie and Barbara knowing it'd be harder to see them once I started treatment.

Henry found an apartment for Nina and me on Franklin Street in San Francisco. It helped to have siblings in real estate. Reta made a name for herself by investing in real estate.

After two days of too much family, Nina and I packed up. We left before Kay arrived to get the children. I did not want Kay and Nina in the same room. "Cats in a bag," I told Ma when she'd suggested they meet. "It'd be like putting two cats in a bag. And I don't want to untangle them."

Our apartment in the City had a bay window overlooking the street. Stores were within walking distance, and Dante's was a ten-minute roll away, three and a half blocks down Franklin and one block over to Broadway. Best of all, there were no hills that Nina needed to push me up. A long walkway led to the front entrance and lobby. On sunny days, Nina waited for me in the garden.

I went to Dante's daily for physiotherapy and to kick morphine. Every time I craved the drug, I drank Ovaltine. Yup, the same Ovaltine of Little Orphan Annie fame. I drank so much I could have gotten dozens of free decoder rings. Two months later, the demon was gone, and I could walk with braces and two canes. I couldn't go far, but I walked.

Financially, I was hurting, however. I'd gone through most of my pension. In March, Winterbottom sent me a letter informing me I'd been cut off from "certain expenditures" and been relieved of Foreign Service now that I was home again. I couldn't blame RCA. I'd been on the dole for almost a year. Their generosity was touching.[115]

In June, I was approved for a pension of $556.00 per year as long as I was permanently disabled—no more RCA paychecks. What I make in a month, I now make in a year. And I still had to pay Kay.

To save money, Nina and I moved from our furnished apartment to Henry's house in Berkeley, which had a room downstairs where we could stay for a few days. After a family conference with Reta, Ed, Henry, and Ma, Reta agreed to loan us her "Villa Grande" on the Russian River for a month so I could truly rest. I hated taking charity, but I couldn't refuse such an offer. It was a beautiful place surrounded by redwoods. Barbara and Georgie could visit when family members came.

My recovery was progressing when another blow struck. In September, the Navy discharged me from the reserves because I was unfit for duty. I must admit the discharge galled me. Not fit for duty! I could still operate radio equipment. I just couldn't do drills—no more monthly stipend from them.

My doctor and family strongly urged me to finish my recovery at the Georgia Warm Springs Foundation, established by President Roosevelt for polio victims.

"George, you are doing so well, able to walk again with canes, and you can type. You'll be back at work in no time. You must go." Ma said.

"Ma, how will I pay for it?"

"Use every penny you have; if they get you back to work, you can start all over again. You are still young."

Nina, ever the optimist, said. "George, so what, we run out of money? I get job as waitress or something. You get better at this place? We go."

My doctor wrote to RCA: "If the patient continues with his present rate of improvement, we believe that he will eventually be in a position to resume a useful status in your organization, but undoubtedly, with a certain percentage of permanent disability, which we hope will be minimal." His letter gave me hope, and I took Ma's advice.

I had a car retrofitted like a motorcycle with a hand brake and accelerator, and I got behind the wheel. I could drive! Nina was terrified of driving, just like Kay. Must be a woman thing.

We packed and once again, I bid my children farewell. They promised to write. I promised to write. Little Barbara held my gaze and said, "Daddy, get better."

Ma said, "Go, George, the children will be fine."

Ma had raised eight children and taken two more under her wing before Georgie and Barbara. Even though she was in her late seventies, she was the mother hen of her brood, taking in the family as they came and went. Knowing my children would be under Ma's watchful eye, helped. I left for Georgia hopeful yet with a heavy heart. This time I listened to Ma.

chapter 21

Warm Springs

1933
Georgia, USA

We arrived at Warm Springs in mid-October, having taken a circuitous route so I could introduce Nina to America. We were thrilled to discover that only my legs were paralyzed, and I gave her a proper honeymoon. We stopped at Yosemite and went to a rodeo. "Real cowboys!" Nina had exclaimed. We celebrated our first wedding anniversary at the Grand Canyon before heading south to Georgia. I sent George and Barbara mementos from each stop, missing them yet grateful for the time alone. For the first time in a long time, I relaxed into each day with a sense of contentment. Nina was an absolute delight, full of wonder, caregiving without complaint, and an understanding lover.

Warm Springs, Georgia, 1933
(George Street Archive)

Warm Springs was a complete surprise. The complex included an indoor hot spring, medical facilities, cabins, and the Meriwether Inn. The hotel was a bit dated but had three stories of porches and windows. Patients lined the porches sitting in chairs and resting in beds. There were no carpets, so that people could wheel without entanglement. Some tables were lower, perfect for wheelchairs. The stairs had railings on each side so I could pull and steady myself. There were ramps for the folks still wheelchair-bound. Best of all, there were people like me. Some were young, some older, women, children, and men in their prime, all broken by the same disease. They were smiling. And I smiled.

"Nina, I think I've died and gone to heaven," I said as we settled into our cabin. "Getting in and out of the hotel and our cabin won't be a struggle. We won't need porters to help me climb stairs. I'll be able to do it myself!"

"We go swim in hot spring every day. Make you better," Nina said. "We go now," and she unpacked our bathing suits.

"*It* will make you better, Nina," I corrected. "Don't forget your subjects and verbs. Our cabin is next to the President's. He's here taking a cure, too. You'll want to speak proper English if we meet him. Besides, a doctor needs to evaluate me before we go to the hot spring. We'll meet with the doctor this afternoon so the center can prescribe a program for me."

My new doctor formulated a plan. It consisted of daily massage, warm spring sessions, walking, and swimming to strengthen my upper body. By the end of the day, I was beat. At first, Nina wheeled me to our evening meal at the hotel. Eventually, I got there under my own power. My table mates celebrated my accomplishments, and I relished the joy of success.

President Roosevelt carved the turkey at our Thanksgiving dinner. We'd seen him about the grounds and at the spring but never had occasion to meet him until now. Aides, secretaries, and security men always surrounded him. However, we briefly chatted at the dinner as he circulated among his guests.

"Mr. President," I said as I extended my hand. "I'm George Street, former RCA Representative in China and Japan. This is my wife, Nina."

Nina said, "Mr. President," shook his hand, and didn't say another word. We'd practiced meeting him when we had learned he'd be in attendance.

"I know your boss well. David and I have lunch at the White House on a regular basis. Did you know that I had a role in creating RCA? I was Secretary of the Navy at the time. When the Great War ended, and it was time to release the companies we'd commandeered for the war effort back to private concerns, I wanted radio to be America-owned—not British-owned. That's when General Electric bought American Marconi and spun off RCA. In fact, that's how I met David Sarnoff. He came with the deal," the President said.

"I was part of the deal too. I worked as an operator at Goat Island in San Francisco Bay."

"Well, I'm delighted to meet you. You obviously moved up in the world if you were a representative in the Orient. Is that where you got polio?"

"Yes, and I told him my story. He was visibly sympathetic when I described the difficulty I had trying to find good medical advice.

"Good God, man. I was at home when I became symptomatic and had the best medical care in the nation," he said. "I can't imagine how horrible that must have been for you."

"It was terrifying at times," I said. "But I remembered your speech. 'The only thing we have to fear is fear itself.' I refused to let fear paralyze me further."

He nodded his head in understanding.

"Trying to get back to the States in a wheelchair was almost as trying," I said. "It took so long to find a ship that could accommodate me that I collected stamps to pass the time. I'd read that you were an avid collector. Would you like some stamps from the newly formed state of Manchukuo?"

"I'd love some. I'll send you a first-issue envelope from the White House when I receive them.[3] Be sure to include your address. Nice meeting you. Stay strong and heal," and he drifted off, greeting his other guests just as warmly.

Meeting the great man was almost as therapeutic as the hot springs. In time, I no longer doubted myself and dismissed the wailings and worries my family had enacted upon me. I viewed my disability as nothing more than an inconvenience that did not limit my mental abilities or my determination and ability to succeed.

I told Nina, who had stood silently at my side while I conversed with FDR, "If a man with polio can be President of the United States, I can certainly make my mark again at RCA."

---

[3] FDR's personal secretary, Louis Howe, sent George a first issue stamp from Vienna dated January 20, 1933. The cover was from The First Austrian Cripple Society, addressed to Mr. President D. Franklin Roosevelt at Hyde Park. *(source: Kathy Klattenhoff)*

FDR carving the turkey at Warm Springs
(FDR Library Photograph Collection NPx 82-71(3).

I studied the President while he made his rounds to learn the art of deflection. When he was photographed standing, he hid his cane behind his back and braced himself against a chair. Head tall. Chest out. He animated his conversation while seated at dinner, and his face became the focal point. No one would have known he had polio. He was a master.

I stayed at Warm Springs as long as money allowed—swimming daily in 88-degree water and working my limbs to keep them flexible. I walked without much pain with the help of crutches, and muscles contoured my arms. Nina never left my side. She was there when I stumbled and there when I swam. I fell in love with her all over again, only this time, it was different. Lust was tamed, but the warmth remained.

By December, my funds were almost depleted, sucked into the pockets of others like so much hot air. I had no regrets. Polio had changed me in unimagined ways, not just physically. I lived each day, really lived it. I tried not to worry, even about money. Where once I'd pinched pennies and fussed over investments, I now spent money to heal and be happy. Warm Springs and Nina had bolstered my crushed ego. I was me again, capable and intelligent, but just a bit different. I had told the American consulate in Japan that I would provide for Nina, and I meant to keep my word. I was obligated to Kay, and did not intend to miss a payment. It was time to work.

I contacted Winterbottom at RCA and told him I was strong enough and well enough to return to part-time work. He invited me to Radio City, Rockefeller Center in New York, RCA's new headquarters. Nina and I packed and hit the road again, stopping only when needed since I could drive longer without getting fatigued. When we arrived, I booked a cheap hotel downtown and was at RCA the next day.

"George, it's good to see you up and about," Winterbottom said when I hobbled in with my canes, head high and my chest out. "You've had a helluva time. RCA appreciates all you've done and regrets the sacrifice you must bear. Your work in the Orient increased our traffic tremendously."

"I'm glad to hear that. I will never forget how RCA helped me through my darkest days. I want to show my appreciation by coming back to work for you. My legs might not work well, but the rest of me is all George Street. I'm ready. I've been keeping abreast of the situation in the Orient through Sheck. It sounds like things are going okay."

Within minutes, he asked me to take over the management of the new branch office in the center, effective 2 January 1934. Surprised, pleased, and encouraged, I agreed even though I was not entirely sure that my body could handle the task.

I telegraphed Ma that I had secured employment in New York and wrote to Georgie and Barbara.

> I am still in New York City. Last week there was a big snowfall, and the weather was very cold. But I stay inside all of the time, so the weather makes little difference to me. Hope you both are doing well in school. After a while, I shall send you an address to write to, and then you can tell me all about yourselves. Here are some of the new US stamps to evenly divide between you both. [116]

Nina and I moved to an apartment close to Radio City and enjoyed being weekend tourists. My work was not demanding—unlike the stress of the Orient. I hinted to Winterbottom that Hawaiian weather would suit me better. Lo and behold, after proving myself in New York, Winterbottom sent me a letter in April, offering me a positon in Honolulu. RCA planned to open a new office in Los Angeles and the current manager of Honolulu wanted to return to his old stomping ground in LA and take the job. I didn't think twice. I got in touch with the RCA's travel planner to work out the timing and details.[117]

In May, I wrote my farewell speech:

> I leave this place without a sigh;

If I stayed here I'd surely die.
Rockefeller's cellar has got my goat:
No more forced air goes down my throat!
I'm on my way to a sunnier clim,
Where balmy breezes waft the vine—
To fair Hawaii where the good old Oke'[118]
Once more will quench my thirsty throat.

chapter 22

Betrayed

1935
SF Bay Area

Nina and I motored to San Francisco to catch a steamer to Honolulu, arriving in eight days. No sightseeing this time. We were Hawaii-bound. I was anxious to see my children. Excited for them to see me. I was confident. Back on my feet—so to speak. I now walked with one cane and braces; I'd gained weight and felt strong.

When I arrived at Ma's house, Georgie and Barbara were not there.

"Ma, where are my children? I thought you'd have them since I telegraphed my arrival time. Is Kay causing problems?

"George, get settled. Henry is coming over for dinner. We'll talk then. Your kids are fine. It's just that things have changed a bit," she said.

"Changed? What's going on? Why didn't you write to me about whatever it is?"

"George, the kids are fine. We'll discuss it later," she replied, then left for the kitchen to help Anna prepare dinner. Anna, her husband—also a George—and their children were living with Ma. George was working, but only minimally. Like Kay, he'd been pounding the pavement to find a better paying job, but the Depression lingered.

Nina lugged our bags up the stairs to a bedroom and stayed out of the way.

When Henry arrived, greetings were short. He made eye contact, and I said, "Henry, Ma said you wanted to talk to me about the children. What's going on?

Ma put the meal on the table. "Dinners ready," she said. Henry removed a chair so I could roll up to the table. Nina sat beside me; the others busied themselves by placing their napkins on their lap and sipping wine. I sat upright and swept the table with my gaze.

"Well?" I said with my hands in my lap.

"This won't be easy to hear," Henry said, and he paced his napkin on the table and turned toward me. "Let me start at the beginning. Kay was caught in bed with a married man."

"What!" I rocked back in the chair and looked at Ma. The others at the table watched their food, perhaps hoping it would mold before their eyes so they could have an excuse to leave.

Henry continued, "It gets worse. His wife grabbed a razor strop and beat Kay on her bare back. God knows what she did to her husband."

"Ma, why didn't you tell me? Good God. How long has this been going on? How could Kay do such a thing? No, I can see Kay being stupid." I took a moment to digest what I'd heard and asked, "What do the children know about it?"

Ma said, "Georgie knows something happened. He's almost thirteen, after all. He told me about putting cold compresses on Kay's back when she came home."

"Why didn't you tell me, Ma? I have half a mind to go to Kay's right now and give her a piece of my mind. Is she still living at her mother's?"

"No, she landed a job in San Francisco and has an apartment there."

Ma took a bite of food and then glanced at Henry.

"Are the children with her? Who watches them after school?" I asked. "What aren't you telling me? Tell me what is going on, goddammit."

Ma swallowed and said defensively, Sometimes they took the ferry, and I met them at the mole. Barbara and Georgie were alone when she was at work. Kay made them a big pot of macaroni and cheese to eat when they came home."

"Why are you speaking in the past tense? What is going on?" Again, there was silence at the table. Not one person looked at me. "I can't believe this."

Ed piped up, "Henry, you started this; now you finish it."

"There's more, George," Henry said.

"More?"

"Yes, there's a lot more."

Ma interjected, "Henry, maybe now is not the right time."

"Oh, it's beyond the right time, Ma, and you know it. George, I just found out. After the Kay incident, Reta, Ed, and Ma took the children and put them in a boarding house in the city."

"What!" I bellowed. I pushed back from the table as a cold vapor wrapped around my heart. Anna and her husband left the table and busied themselves in the kitchen. Ed chewed his food noisily.

"My children are in a boarding house? A boarding house? Where? How could you allow this to happen? I trusted you, Ma. Why wasn't I told? I put my head in my hands and slumped in my chair then, straightened, my anger giving me strength.

"I can't believe this," I spat. "I have wanted custody of Georgie and Barbara since the divorce. Ma, you know that. How could you do this and not tell me? I'm perfectly capable. I have a job and a wife. How could you?"

Ma said, "Settle down, George. We were just trying to do our best, given your current situation and Kay's complete lack of decency. How could you and Nina have taken care of them with your illness? Nina is barely older than a child. Besides, how could you afford them?"

I shifted my legs and stood, cane in hand, the hurt from Ma's betrayal worse than the pain from my polio. Bile rose to my chest. Nina put her hand on my arm. She'd sat in stiff silence the entire time. What must she think of my family?

"I have never missed a support payment. Nina has been a God-send. Don't you dare say unkind things about her. She knows how to trust and be trusted, unlike you. I can't believe you put them in a boarding house and didn't tell me. How long have they been there?"

Ma crumpled and said, "About a year. I was just trying to do what was best. Obviously, Kay was an unfit mother. You are unwell. What was I to do?"

"The entire time I was in New York? Why didn't the children mention it in their letters?" I sat down, suppressing panic.

"I told them not to write about anything that would upset you, and Mrs. Scott, the boarding house owner, read their letters before she posted them. She was instructed to have them rewrite them if they hinted at their situation."

"On top of everything else, you censored their letters. Unbelievable. How will I ever trust you again? Some family!"[119] I said as my heart crunched like a baked shell on a hot beach. I stood again, unable to quell my rising anger.

"Henry, what's your excuse?"

"I had nothing to do with it. I just found out. Don't take your irritation out on me. Sit down, and let's figure out what to do next."

I sat. Stunned. My heart raced, and my hands shook. I don't think I've ever been so enraged. It was raw and blistering. Kay had pushed me to the brink several times, but never sent me over a cliff as Reta, Ed, and Ma had done.

"George, I'm so sorry. I thought I was helping you, protecting you, protecting them." Ma said.

"Protecting me? From what? My children? Or was this yours and Reta's and Ed's way of saying that you didn't think I had a chance in hell at success? What kind of mother does that?"

Henry said, "You have every right to be angry. Reta and Ed were out of line."

"Reta and Ed? So was Ma. I know Reta's husband is an attorney, but how dare they? Why aren't my children in the house I purchased for you, Ma?"

"I bought it from you," Ma said stiffly. "It's not your house. Anna and her family needed a place to stay. There just wasn't enough room if George and Barbara stayed. I figured that if the kids were in San Francisco, then Kay would be able to see them more."

"Kids! Kids! My children are not goats! Although you've treated them like animals. So Anna and her family are more important than my children? What makes you think you had any right to make these decisions on my behalf?"

Ma rallied, angry at me—and herself, "You gave me a power of attorney when you left for the Orient and then New York. I had every right. You certainly weren't there for them while you gallivanted about with Nina. Don't you blame me. Given your circumstances, I tried to do what was best for your children. I thought you'd understand."

"I don't understand why you never consulted me. Being a cripple does not mean you have the right to take my children and not tell me. I've been in the States for over a year. I'm gainfully employed. I've never missed a support payment, even when I was in dire straits. Who gets my payments now?"

"Reta made arrangements with the boarding school, and the money goes directly to them. Kay gets what's left." Ma said.

"You've got it all figured out, don't you? Jesus, what kind of family does such a thing?"

I turned to Nina, "Pack our bags. I do not want to stay one more minute in this house. We'll get a hotel."

"You can stay with me," Henry offered."

"Did you have any part of this?" I snapped.

"No, I already told you. I just found out about it and insisted you be told."

Ma rose, her eyes swimming with tears, "He's correct, George. Henry thought it a terrible idea to keep it from you. I'm so sorry. I didn't want to bother you with all the details for fear that you'd relapse or something."

"You think this is better, Ma?" I shook my head and crumpled into my chair. Ma came to my side. I said, "Do not try to comfort me. Stay away. How could you? Reta and Ed have always been bullies— always thought they knew best. But you? I trusted you. This is beyond belief. Henry, can we leave? I can't be here one more second.

"Nina," I yelled. "Get our luggage. We're leaving now."

Nina hustled upstairs, threw our stuff in suitcases, and carried it down.

"Goodbye, Mother," she said as she headed for the door. "Thank you for the meal."

I said, "Thank you for nothing, Ma. I don't know if I can ever forgive you. My children. You allowed Ed and Reta to take my children, and you didn't say a word."

Henry took my arm to help me navigate the eight stairs to the sidewalk lined with our luggage. My legs were as shaky as boiled noodles, and Nina helped me into the front seat while Henry loaded the bags. Ma and Anna stood at the door, silent. When I made eye contact, Ma burst into tears.

"Some family," I said. "How dare you?"

The Street clan at Bates Street. Barbara is front row third from the left. George Jr. is in the second row between Nina and Grandma Street. *(George Street Archive)*

chapter 23

"Some Family"

1935
SF Bay Area

The next day, Henry filled me in. Nina and I sat in his breakfast nook drinking coffee, the steam curling from our cups disappearing into thin air. Nina stood to set the table for breakfast. Last night I was so upset I couldn't even talk to her about my family's actions. I barely slept worrying about the children.

"Henry, what do you know," I asked after taking a sip.

"When Kay got a job in San Francisco, things fell apart. She rented a walk-up, and shuffled Barbara and Georgie between Ma, Louise, Reta, and her mother. Kay would promise Barbara and Georgie that she'd take them to the movies or the park and never show up to get them. You could see the disappointment on little Barbara's face. It just broke Ma's heart."

"Jesus, how could Kay do that to her children? I don't know if I should be angrier at her or Ma. When did Reta and Ed take them?"

"Shortly after you left for New York. According to Reta, Kay was a mess, bruised from her beating and adjusting to a job that kept her on her feet all day. Adding children to the mix was too much for her. Kay was tired after work and would slap some food on the table and leave the kids to fend for themselves. On weekends she'd farm them out so she could go on the prowl. In her defense, you know Kay needed someone to look out for her. How did you expect her to take care of herself much less the children? Reta stepped in, and Kay lost it. Reta knew a couple of women who ran a boarding house and made the arrangements for Barbara and Georgie to settle there. "

"Geez, Kay could never stand up to Reta and Ed."

"Kay made a fuss, but in the end let them take control of the situation. Don't be too hard on Reta and Ed. Their intentions were good."

"I still can't believe Ma went along with everything and never said a word."

"You were in New York and she worries about you. She disapproves of Nina. I think she hopes you'll leave her. Ma loves your kids and she hated seeing them shuffled around."

"She must not think very highly of me if she thinks I could leave Nina after all she's done for me. I don't understand why the children never said anything in their letters. Why Ma didn't."

"I asked the same question. Ma coached them not to say anything. She told them it would upset you and make you sicker and she really believed that. That is why she didn't come right out and tell you."

"You're darn right it would have upset me. Kay too?" I asked. "Was she sworn to secrecy?"

"Probably. Kay was afraid of Ed and Reta, afraid they wouldn't give her the remainder of your support payments."

My stomach lurched as I tried to wrap my head around my family's betrayal. "You didn't know?" I asked Henry wanting confirmation after the heated argument of yesterday.

He shook his head, "They never said a word to me. They probably knew I'd blow the whistle on them. When you think about it wasn't a bad solution. The children were in a stable environment within visiting distance of their mom, and Kay was freed from a responsibly she never could handle."

"Well, this is going to end," I said, slamming the tip of my cane on the floor. "I feel like a father whose wife sold his daughter to a geisha house without telling him. I've got a couple of weeks before my ship leaves for Honolulu. How do I get custody of them? I never should have left them with Kay. I should never have trusted Ma. How could I have been so naïve?"

"George, there is no doubt that Ma was wrong but you asked too much of her. Don't be so hard on her. Good God, she's 78 and without a husband. You did give her Power of Attorney, and I'm sure she thought what she did was in their best interest. I know she was also worried about your recovery and ability to care for them."

"I don't get it. Why didn't Ma move them in with her after Kay's escapade?" I asked.

"I asked. She explained that Anna and her family needed a place to stay. The Great Depression left them without work or a place to live. Ma said having so many in the house was too much for her. Anna and her husband were in one bedroom, their children in the other. Georgie and Barbara slept on the floor in the living room, and she had all those mouths to feed."

"So Anna's family was more important than my children that she'd agreed to watch over? I would have sent my support payments to her to help out. All she had to do was ask."

"Don't place the blame on Ma. You never asked her how she was managing. She's tired. She's also a mother. Mothers take care of their children. Well, most do. You can't put this all on her. Look to yourself too."

"What was I supposed to do? I have a job, children to support, and a career to build. I didn't intend to get polio. I thought I had a family I could rely upon. Obviously, that was my mistake."

"Don't go feeling sorry for yourself or blaming others. You made your choices. You chose yourself over your children. What is done is done, and you've paid a terrible price."

We both glanced at my legs, knowing I'd never walk again without assistance. His words stabbed my smoldering heart, and I slipped into a hot, hollow silence. I turned and stood at the window, studying the coiling clouds while I tried to clear my head. Henry was right. I'd prioritized my career over my children. I'd put myself first. I'd hidden in a shroud of "if onlys" and "what ifs" instead of facing reality. In my gut I know Kay wasn't capable, and I'd relied upon others to pick up the pieces of our shattered family. The realization stung. But my path forward cleared.

"You're right," I said. "I made a terrible mistake. But no more. I'm perfectly capable. I can run errands, cook, work, and drive. It's more than Kay did. She never learned to drive or cook. George and

Barbara will be better off with me. How do I get custody of them? I'll show this family what I'm made of."

"I'm a real estate attorney, but I'll look into it."

"Well, I'm stopping my support payments. I'll be damned if I am going to play Ed and Reta's game. Besides, it might expedite a new custody hearing."

"That good idea," Nina interjected. She hadn't said a word up to this point. She didn't need to; her facial expression spoke for her. "I tell you no pay, Kay. She not take care of children, ever."

"Nina, stop. This is not your concern. I am going to get my children and take care of them. If you want to help, great. If you don't, leave."

Henry said, "I think stopping support payments would be considered child abandonment."

"I'm doing it. I'll talk to whatever lawyer you recommend. The way I see it, Reta, Ed, and Ma kidnapped my children. They may not have approved of Kay's behavior, but they had no right to take them away from her without my consent. I'm fixing this."

I called Kay after Henry left to meet with a lawyer. The phone rang three times before she picked up.

"Hello?" she said tentatively. Phones and radio baffled her, yet she believed in fortune tellers. Ghosts could talk to her but pulses through the ether were beyond her. She never grasped the physics of wave technology no matter how much I tried to explain it to her.

"Kay, this is George.

"Oh, George, it's so good to hear from you. You sound like you are right next to me. Can you hear me okay? You've been gone so long. Can I see you? I have a job now."

"So I heard. Where are my children?" I asked. I had no desire for chitchat. She sidestepped my question like I expected.

"Maybe I can bring them to your mother's house this weekend," she offered. "Reta told me you were here and doing better. The Fortune Teller said so, too."

"I'm delighted to hear that a mystic told you that. Geez, Kay. Put Georgie on the phone. I want to talk to him," I said, not falling for her evasiveness. I wanted her to give her enough rope so she could hang herself.

"He's not here right now."

"Well, how about Barbara?"

"She's not here either."

"Where are they? It's almost bedtime, and it's a school day."

Silence.

"Kay, where are the children?" I knew she was twisting in the wind now.

"George, it's not my fault. Ed and Reta took them," and she burst out crying.

"Henry told me all about it, Kay. About your affair. About your beating. About Georgie and Barbara being placed in a boarding house. All of it. Have you no shame? What kind of mother are you? To have given up your children? Did you even think about how doing so would upset them and me?

"Don't be so mean. What was I supposed to do? It wasn't my fault. He took me to lunch. We drank too much. His wife was supposed to be out. He was a wolf. And you weren't there to protect me."

"So it's all *my* fault because I wasn't there to drag you home like I did at company parties. You are unbelievable, absolutely unbelievable. I'm not going to waste my time even talking about this. I want to know why my children are in a boarding house."

"You left us! You left me! What was I supposed to do? Reta and Ed were so angry. They said they'd have me thrown in jail or something. That I'd be on the street," she said through sobs.

"So it's all my fault again? You had my address in New York. Why didn't you send me a telegram? Was that too much trouble? Would the cost have kept you from buying a new dress?

"I tried. I got a job because your payments weren't enough. The only one I found was in the City, and Mother needed to rent my room. I love Georgie and Barbara. I tried. I really tried."

"You think sleeping around was good for them? How about putting them in a boarding house? How did that help them? I can never forgive you for this. I'm going to get custody of the children, and you will never see them again. I will get them as far away from you as possible, so they won't learn your evil ways. And don't expect another dime out of me. I am done with you." I hung up on her, slamming the handset into the cradle.

I braced myself against the wall, drained, heartbroken, and sick to my stomach. I had to lie down so Nina helped me upstairs. She was happy to hear about my cutting-off payments. She'd never understood why I sent money to Kay, anyway.

The next day I pounded away at the typewriter and put everything in writing for the attorney Henry recommended. Then I called Ed. And I did not mince words.

"Ed, this is George."

"George, can you hear me okay."

"Loud and clear. Good because you better listen up. I'm cutting off my support payments and petitioning for custody of the children. Henry and I will meet with an attorney tomorrow. I have half a mind to charge you and Reta with kidnapping."

"George, don't be stupid. You left knowing Kay was not a good mother. How can you possibly take care of them with polio?"

"Just watch me, Ed, just watch me. I might need canes and braces, but I do just fine. RCA saw fit to promote me, and you think I can't manage? I'll see you in court if I have to." I slammed down the handset, hoping it didn't crack. The phone was getting quite the workout, lately. How dare he imply that I couldn't take proper care of my children?

After we met with the attorney, I found out that Reta, Ed, or Ma would have to pay the boarding house once I stopped payments since they were the ones who signed for Georgie and Barbara. I was tempted to let them. Why make it easier on them after all they'd done? I'm sure they'd be rattled once they found out even though I planned on footing the bill.

The next day Ed called Henry. "Is George there?" he demanded.

Waving his hand at me to be quiet, Henry lied, "I think he's gone to the City on business."

"I'm going to have him taken off the ship if I don't have time to get an injunction against him for child abandonment," Ed said.

"Well, brother, try that only after you get finished with me because I will fight you with all I have to prevent such a thing. Just leave George alone!"[120] And the phone got another slamming. Good thing it was made out of metal.

I spent the rest of the day planning a strategy. I discovered that once I left the mainland, California would have no jurisdiction over my case since Hawaii was a territory. According to my attorney, the easiest way to get custody was to persuade Kay to relinquish them to me.

I called Kay and arranged to meet her for lunch the next day. I did not want to see her. It would take all I could muster not to light into her. She was like a petulant child, expecting other people to take care of her, to love her because of her beauty, the way her grandfather had. Well, she was going to learn otherwise.

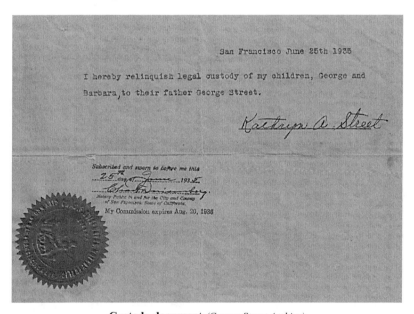

San Francisco June 25th 1935

I hereby relinquish legal custody of my children, George and Barbara, to their father George Street.

Kathryn A. Street

Custody document *(George Street Archive)*

We met at Fisherman's Wharf, a short walk from Kay's work-place at Fort Mason. I could tell she'd dressed to impress me. She wore her fur-collared coat, and it wasn't cold. Her heels tapped the hardwood floor as she walked up.

"George, darling, I love seeing you again," she said. "You look almost the same." She extended her arm and jiggled her bracelet in a blatant attempt for a complement.

I lead the way to a table away from the tourists and the bar. I could tell Kay expected me to help her with her chair and coat. I sat and put my cane on the back of my chair, leaving her standing. She turned full circle, glancing at the diners as though to say, "How dare he!"

"Would you like a drink?" I asked, knowing she would. It galled me even to ask, but experience taught me that she'd fuss if I didn't. A stiff martini is what I needed.

We ordered, and when the drinks arrived, she seductively pulled the olive off the toothpick with her teeth. I rolled my eyes. She was unbelievable!

"Kay, stop all your nonsense. It's not going to work on me. I visited with Georgie and Barbara before I came here. They seem well, but they miss you. When was the last time you were with them?"

"Oh, I don't know. I've been so busy working. It's exhausting. It's hard to find the time. I talk to Georgie and Barbara on the phone and write them notes."

"Well, Barbara told me you promised to see them, and then you'd never show up. Do you understand how that makes them feel? They'd get ready and wait for you. How could you leave them sitting there waiting? Barbara feels that somehow it's her fault you don't want to see them. Georgie doesn't understand. You are their mother, for God's sake."

"I try. I tell them I love them every time I call. They ask to see *your* mother, but I don't feel welcome at her home. What am I supposed to do?"

"You should have thought of that before you slept with a married man. Don't blame my family for not wanting you around after your little escapade. You know how tight laced they are."

"George, it wasn't my fault. I had too much to drink, and he took advantage. He was such a bear.

"Kay, it was wrong, and you know it. It takes two."

"I only wanted to be loved a little bit."

"There is no such thing as a little bit of sex," I said.

She blushed, gasped, and turned her head, seemingly embarrassed by my crudeness. I knew better. She used the power that dwelled between her legs to get what she wanted. She was a blond bear trap. Her vanity, her desire to be "kept," never changed. She was all about clothes, appearances, and flirting. She was like a leaf floating in a stream, waiting for a branch to catch and hold her.

"Kay, I'm not here to talk about you," taking a deep breath to calm myself. "I want to talk about the children. Their situation is intolerable. I've always said I wanted custody. Now I'm going to sue for it. You can make it easy, or you can make it hard. It's obvious you can't take proper care of them and bring them up in a moral environment. Where were they when you were rolling around in the hay? How many men have you had over to your place? Any judge in his right mind will label you as an unfit mother."

"I never had men over when they were there! What do you think I am?" she said. "How could you ask such a thing?" Several diners craned their heads to watch the show, but this time it wasn't out of a desire to see a lovely woman. She stood in a huff full of righteous indignation with her nose in the air, head titled away from me. I told her to sit.

"Kay, please don't make a scene. If you do, the next call you will get will be from an attorney, and you'll have to spend your dress money paying a bill that is not necessary. Calm down."

"You don't understand," she said. "I can't make enough money to support me, Georgie, and Barbara. You want the kids to have a fine home, and expect me to make it happen. You haven't been around for over two years. What about that? Where were you? Gallivanting all over the Orient with some floozy you'd found at a club. At least I came from a good family. As you said, it takes two— two to properly raise children. I did my best." She dabbed at her eyes and glanced around to see who was watching, visually inviting them to watch. She was good at embarrassing me in public.

I was determined to keep control of the situation. "Kay," I said as I took her hands from across the table, "we have both made mistakes. I expected to be gone for six months, and things got complicated. I went so I could make your support payments after I was laid off. I certainly didn't expect to get polio."

"The fortune teller knew. She told me something bad was going to happen."

"The fortune teller again. Have you asked her what you should do now?"

"Yes, she said things were cloudy. She didn't know."

"Well, I know what we need to do. We must think about what is best for Georgie and Barbara. Children don't wait to grow up while their parents get their lives on track."

Kay nodded, wiping the tears from her eyes, "They have grownup so fast. Oh, George, why don't we take care of the children together, again? Don't you think it'd be best for them to have us both? A mother and a father? I'll let you take me back. I've been so lost without you. I promise I will be the mother and wife you want."

"It won't work. I'm married to Nina. Just like before, you and I would be at each other's throats in no time. We are too different. I made a mistake in marrying you. You were never meant to be a wife, much less a mother. You still aren't." I wanted to say more, but doing so would serve no purpose.

She reared back like a snake, ready to strike. "How dare you?" she said. "Do you think I had an easy time living with you? All you wanted was a slave, someone to bed whenever you wanted, clean up after you, and raise your children. You promised me the world and gave me nothing." She stuck her nose into the air, aware of her public. "*I* want nothing to do with *you*," she said, acting like Tallulah Bankhead in a romance movie, getting in the last word to save face.

"Good. That's fine with me. Let's talk about the children. Georgie and Barbara will be teenagers soon. How will you handle that when you act like one yourself? Or do you expect to keep them in a boarding house until they reach twenty-one? I am prepared to keep them. I have an estate agent looking for a house in Honolulu. Nina has agreed to be their stepmother. You will be free of worry, and the Streets will no longer be a part of your life. I will no longer be a part of your life. All you have to do is sign a paper saying you give me custody."

"If you take them to Honolulu, I will never see them again. Oh, my little Georgie and Barbara. What will I do? My babies."

"They are not babies anymore. They are children who need a steady hand to become adults. I will give you money so you can visit them," I said, knowing that money always worked with Kay. I'd book her at a hotel to minimize contact, if she did come. She'd probably spend the money on clothes anyway.

"That might work," she said.

"I will also cover the cost of George and Barbara's boarding house until I send for them since I'm no longer giving you support payments. God knows I wouldn't want Ed and Reta to foot their bill. The price would be too high. You must understand that the money I will give you is a gift, not support money, not a bribe—simply a gift. I will never make a second offer. This will be it, Kay."

"How will I survive?"

"Oh, I'm sure you'll figure something out. There are plenty of men around. At least you won't have to worry about the children anymore."

"What a thing to say. You are so crass. But you're right; there are lots of nice, kind men out there, unlike you. Men who appreciate a woman like me," she said and she wiggled her bracelet. "I don't know why I ever dreamed we could get back together. When will you give me the money?" she asked all semblance of flirtation gone.

"After this is settled and the children are on a boat to Honolulu," I said.

With that incentive—and much drama—she agreed to accompany me across the street to a notary. Her tears stained the page when she signed over custody. She left without a word and hailed a cab. I hoped I'd never have to see her again. I expected her to call Ed and Reta to let them know what we'd agreed upon and to say a few choice words about me. I did not care. I was drained. Battle-scarred and a little worried. Children. I had to raise children, but there was no way I'd back away from that responsibility. Not now. Not after what my family had done to me. I'd show them. Now, all that remained was the ratification of the new custody agreement.

After talking to my attorney, I left Kay's money with Henry and told him I'd wire him when it was time to hand it over to Kay. Henry promised to keep an eye on things so Nina and I could proceed to Honolulu. I imagined Ed dreaming up all kinds of nefarious plots. He'd learn soon enough that he no longer had control.

chapter 24

Aloha

1935
SF Bay Area

The next day, I drove to San Francisco to visit the children and tell them what was happening. I made an appointment with the boarding house proprietor and confirmed that the street wasn't steep so that I could negotiate it alone. Getting in and out of the car without assistance was a chore even with help. I wanted to talk to the children without Nina and left her to do the laundry and ironing before we packed.

The sky was the color of denim, the air soft with moisture as I made my way across the bay on the ferry. I stayed in the car worrying over what to say, visualizing a life with them. The children were old enough to handle the truth, and God knows they deserved it.

After rumbling off the ferry and negotiating the City's steep streets, I parked in front of the boarding house on Pacific Avenue. I set the hand brake so the car wouldn't roll and exited when there was a break in the traffic. Leaving the door open into the traffic lane for any length of time was dicey, but I had no choice. I used the rope handles I'd had installed to the frame to pull myself upright once I'd swung my legs out.

I'd learned the hard way to carry two canes. Propped on the passenger seat, I pulled them within easy reach. I'd use two canes if the roadbed were steep, potholed, or slippery. Today was a one- cane day.

I slid one cane forward, braced against the car, and stabilized my legs. Keeping one hand on the hood after closing the door, I stepped up the curb and faced the house. A patch of yellow wood sorrel cracked the sidewalk.

Stairs. The house was a half-story above street level. I forgot to ask about stairs. Fortunately, there was a sturdy railing.

I shifted my cane to my left hand and pulled myself forward on the handrail one step at a time. I had to take a breather at the top. I tugged on my shirt sleeve to make sure my tattoo was covered, then swung the door knocker several times. The grilled peek hole slid open.

"You must be George Sr. I'm Mrs. Green." I took a step back, and the heavy oak door swung open. "I see the resemblance in Barbara," Mrs. Green said. "Please come in. This is Mrs. Scott, my widowed sister. She assists me with the borders." Turning toward the buxom woman, I extended my hand.

"Would you care for some tea?" Mrs. Green asked.

"Thank you, yes."

While she put the kettle on, Mrs. Scott offered me a seat in the parlor. I sat, grateful for the respite after the stairs. When I settled, tea in hand, I explained that I had recently returned from the Orient and came to see my children. I asked, "How many boarders do you have?"

"Right now, we have a couple in the basement unit and Barbara and George on the top floor next to our rooms."

"This house is a grand old lady," I remarked as I took in the Victorian wainscoting. The richness of the era was still evident throughout, velvet curtains, parquet floors, and rich, mahogany wood trim.

"This is our family home. Fortunately, we didn't lose it in the 1906 earthquake."

"My goodness," I said. "It still has gas lighting. You don't see that very often."

"Yes, we couldn't afford to upgrade. I taught George Jr. how to light and turn them off. Barbara is not allowed to touch them. We wouldn't want to start a fire, now would we?"

"Do they share a room?" George just graduated from elementary school. He seemed a bit old to be housed with his sister.

"Their rooms have adjoining sliding doors that are only open during the day when they study. We keep a very close eye on them."

"Where do they play? Is there a yard?"

"There's a small one at the back of the house, and there are parks. Barbara prefers to play dolls on the roof deck, which is fenced, of course. We are within walking distance of the Presidio. George Jr.'s school is down the hill, just a couple of blocks away."

"And the only other people in this big old house are a couple in the basement? What does he do for a living?" I asked, wanting to be sure the children would be safe until I could send for them. Adults had not treated them kindly, of late. Reta had assured me that Mrs. Green and Mrs. Scott were good people, and my first impression was positive, but I wanted to be sure.

"Yes, they are the only other boarders, have been for years. They keep to themselves. She cleans houses and is not around during the day. He is unemployed at present, but he takes the street car to the Embarcadero and sifts through the dredged muck for placer gold. He's found several grams and has never been late with his rent."[121]

"How enterprising," I remarked. "You may have been unaware, but I have provided the funds for George and Barbara's board. I am headed to Honolulu soon and they will join me. I will continue to pay their board until I send for them at the end of the school year. I would like to see them and let them know my plans. Are they upstairs?"

"Oh," said Mrs. Green visibly taken aback. "Reta never mentioned they'd be going with you to Honolulu."

"Well, they are my children now. Kay has signed over custody. I expect the court to ratify it any day now."

"My goodness, how things change. I will need paperwork before I release them," said Mrs. Green.

"Certainly, my attorney will send it to you."

"I'll get them," Mrs. Scott offered. "No need for you to climb the stairs." She hurried up the wide wooden steps, gathering her skirt so she wouldn't trip. I heard a door open and close. Then Barbara and George clamored down sounding, like a herd of elephants. Mrs. Scott was close on their heels.

"Daddy!" Barbara exclaimed as she rushed into my arms. Georgie was too dignified for such an emotional outburst, but I could tell he was happy to see me.

"We'll let you be," Mrs. Green said, and she and Mrs. Scott left the room. The children perched in their vacated chairs.

"Look at you. You've grown so much! I'm so happy to see you again. Do you like it here?" I asked.

"I wish Mother were here," Barbara said.

"George?"

"It's okay. Not as much fun as the YMCA camp you sent me to last summer. I miss woodshop. I didn't get to finish the table I was making for Grandma, but I don't have to walk so far to school now. I'm in Boy Scouts, too. We meet at the San Francisco City Hall, and Mrs. Green takes me there."

"It sounds like you are keeping busy. Is the food good? You both look healthy," I said.

"Oh yes, the food is much better than what Mother cooked," Barbara admitted.

"Good. That's good."

"Can we go live with Grandma again?" Barbara asked.

"Well, what would you say about coming to live with me in Hawaii?"

Barbara and Georgie both took a moment before responding. Barbara was the first to speak up, "Where's Hawaii?" She asked.

"It's a group of islands in the middle of the ocean, a five-day sail on a ship. The islands are much bigger than the ones in the bay. There are palm trees and turtles and beaches with black sand!" Her eyes brightened, and a smile crept across her face.

"Turtles?"

"Yes, great big sea turtles."

"Really?" Georgie asked. "We could live with you on an island?"

"Yes."

"Why is the sand black?" Barbara asked.

"Because of the volcanoes," I said. "You will learn all about it in school."

"There are schools on an island?"

"Yes, and parks, and grocery stores and movies, just like here."

I then gave them the rundown, explaining that their mother couldn't care for them and Grandma had a house full. I eliminated the uglier details. They were quiet, not sure what to believe.

"Turtles? I want to see the turtles," Barbara said. Georgie remained still and silent.

"It's my turn to take care of you. Nina will be your new mother —your stepmother. How about that?"

Georgie offered, "I have a friend who has a stepmother. I guess it'll be okay.

"Well, I can't wait for us to be a family," I said. "I've wanted this for so long. Come here, both of you," and I held them tight. "No more macaroni and cheese, no more disappointments. We'll have a fine house and go to the beach a lot."

Barbara pulled free and asked, "Will our home be on the beach?"

"We'll see. We have to find a house first. Nina and I are sailing for Honolulu aboard the *SS Mariposa* in a couple of days, so we can have our little grass shack ready for you when you come. When we leave, Grandma will bring you to the pier to wave *aloha* to our big white ship."

Barbara asked. "You are leaving without us?" I could see the fear in her eyes. How I hated to say goodbye once again. How would she learn to trust again? Kay not showing up when she said she would.

Ma throwing her out of her room. Ed and Reta putting her in a boarding house. Me leaving. Georgie was her only anchor, and he was still a child.

"We are not saying goodbye," I said. "We are saying aloha. Aloha means hello *and* goodbye. Wave aloha, and you will see me soon—in paradise. I promise."

When it was time for me to leave, I said "aloha" to the children as they waved from the porch. "I'll call you every day until I leave," I said, "and I'll send a wireless when we arrive. I promise. You will know where I am every step of the way."

chapter 25

Settled

1935
Honolulu, Territory of Hawaii

Within days, Nina and I boarded our ship for Honolulu. My leave was over, and I didn't dare ask for an extension after all RCA had done for me. Henry and Ma drove us to the pier and picked up Georgie and Barbara so they could see us off. After paying a porter to take our luggage on board, I said to them, "You will be on a ship just like this one. Finish your schooling. Mrs. Green and Mrs. Scott will take good care of you, and soon you will be in paradise with us."

Barbara pressed her face into me and hugged me tightly. Her hat fell off but I couldn't catch it before it hit the ground. We let it be until Nina pulled her from me and placed it on her head. Georgie shook my hand and I pulled him to an embrace. For a moment, I held him. Nina stepped forward and gave them a peck on the cheek.

"*Aloha*," I told Georgie and Barbara as I gave each a final farewell hug. "We will be together soon."

"*Aloha*, Daddy," Barbara said and Georgie just nodded his head.

I left with a heavy heart—exhausted from the stress, worried about Kay wanting to back out. I think she wanted to be a good mother but she just didn't know how. I turned to wave again once we'd made our way onto the gangway. Barbara jumped up and down when she spotted me at the rail and waved with both hands. Georgie raised an arm. Seeing them lifted my spirits and in that moment I knew I'd done the right thing. And I was settled—steaming forward with the wind in my face, leaving the past in my wake, heading for "*Aloha*."

No police officers tried to remove me from the ship in San Francisco or when we stopped in Los Angeles before crossing to Honolulu. My attorney put a stop to that. RCA paid for our first class passage, and Nina and I spent our time discussing plans for the children.

First we discussed Nina's choices—she could go on her own, or help me raise my children. I'd made it perfectly clear the children were my priority.

"Barbara help cook," she said. "I teach how to run house. We be happy family. I take good care of Georgie and Barbara while you work."

"Georgie and I will work on a project together. He said he made several things in wood shop and he liked working with tools. We must keep them busy, so they won't miss Kay too much."

"That no problem," Nina said. "They not miss Kay. She no good."

We docked in Honolulu on Barbara's eleventh birthday, June 3rd. I had the purser send her a radiogram with birthday wishes and a promise that she'd be in Hawaii soon. While I waited for the crowd to disburse before attempting the gangway with my braces and cane, reporters from the *Honolulu Star-Bulletin* and *Advertiser* snapped a picture of Nina and me for their articles headlined, *"New RCA Chief Here for Duty."* Nina was fetching in her wide-brimmed hat and orchard leis. I stood chest out with my cane behind my back. I asked for a copy so I could send it to Barbara and George Jr. I had made them a promise and was determined to keep it so they could trust again.

George and Nina Street 1935 *(George Street Archive)*

chapter 26

Launched

1935
Honolulu, Territory of Hawaii

My real estate agent located a two-bedroom, one-bath house with a maid's quarters one block from Hunakai Beach. When we inspected the house, the gravelly sound of receding waves caught my attention. A warming breeze carried the scent of oleander, and palms rattled overhead. We couldn't see the beach from the house, but we could hear and feel it. I smiled as the agent led us down the short concrete walkway to the front door. It was level, solid, and easy to navigate. There was only one porch step. Perfect. And there were no stairs in the house. The bathroom separated the two bedrooms, and the living room opened to the kitchen. A lanai stretched across the back of the house. It was perfect.

Nina said, "Georgie sleep in maid's quarters. Barbara sleep back bedroom."

"Yes, he can use the bathroom in the carport. I think we found our home. It's perfect."

Within steps of the front door, there was a bus stop and an access alley to the beach. Nina loved the house as much as I did, so we purchased 4604 Kahala Avenue within days of our arrival. I immediately sent a radiogram to Georgie and Barbara, telling them we had found our "little grass shack" within walking distance of the beach.

One of the first pieces of mail I received at our new address was a letter from California's childcare bureau demanding this, that, and everything else. Ed was stirring up trouble again, I surmised. I contacted my attorney, who wired that the court had ratified our new custody arrangement, but word hadn't trickled back to the childcare agent. The children were mine. I was in charge now. Nina and I had a lot to get done before their arrival.

I sent a letter to the children letting them know they'd be on a big ship at the end of the school year, off to a tropical island for a great adventure.

I sent Ma a radiogram and arranged a time for a call because phoning the mainland costs two dollars a minute. I wanted to be sure she'd be home.

"Ma, this is George. Can you hear me?

"Yes. I hear you fine. It's like you are right next to me. Can you hear me?"

"Yes, just fine. I'm calling to let you know that I now have legal custody of the children. I appreciate all you have done for them in the past, but you will no longer have to worry about them. I have bought a house, and purchased passage for them on the *SS Lurline*. They will live with Nina and me in Honolulu in a fortnight."

There was a long pause. What could Ma say?

"Tell me about the house," she said.

I hesitated. Why should Ma care after she put my children in a boarding house? I said, "It's a lot nicer than the last place they lived." And I described it in detail, telling her where the children would sleep, about the bus stop, and the beach.

"I hope it works out," she said. "I realize we did a terrible thing, and I hope you will find it in your heart to forgive me someday. I love them and want the best for both. May I write to Georgie and Barbara?"

"Yes, but not too often. It will be important for them to know you care, but I don't want you mooning about how much you miss them. They are very fond of you, but they need to forget so they won't be scarred by what you did."

"Oh, I'm so sorry. I should never have listened to Ed and Reta."

"I wish you hadn't, too. I've got to hang up now. This call is costing a bloody fortune. Henry is going to tell Ed and Reta for me. I want nothing more to do with them. I'm going to hang up now. Give me time, Ma. Goodbye."

"Goodbye, George. I love you." I listened as she slowly replaced the hand piece into the cradle, conflicted about my feelings toward her, wondering if I could ever forgive.

The next morning, I rolled over in the new double bed Nina had bought, grateful we were sleeping together again. It wasn't easy for me to shift positions without help. I had to turn my upper body and then, using my back and hip muscles, lift my right leg and place it on top of my left. I rose on my elbow and stared at Nina sleeping. She had been broken once, abandoned by her family, terrified and helpless in a foreign country. She had survived. Georgie and Barbara could survive, too. Nina wasn't perfect. The children would undoubtedly test her temper and trigger her jealousy. Neither of us had any experience raising children, but now at least they would have a proper home.

She stirred, and I bent and kissed her. I shifted my legs, pushed myself up, and sat. There was no sense in worrying. We'd take it a day at a time.

"George, you work today?" Nina asked.

"Yes, I want to go in early. Tom is going to debrief me before the staff arrives."

"I help put on suit and cook you nice breakfast."

I tugged off my pajama bottoms, slipped on the fresh underwear Nina handed me and strapped on my braces. I cinched them tight. I didn't want to have to make adjustments at the office. Nina lifted my legs one at a time and helped me step into my suit trousers. She threaded my belt, left the buckle open for me to tighten, and gave me a squeeze.

"I can take it from here," I told her. "You go cook breakfast. Bacon would be nice."

I put on a starched, long-sleeved shirt to hide my scarred tattoo. Buttoned, I stood. The braces held me firmly. My cane kept me steady.

After breakfast, I gave Nina a bunch of cash and told her to finish furnishing the house.

"I buy not fancy. I buy used for Barbara and George Jr."

"There's an ad in the *Advertiser* about a moving sale. Take a cab and see what they have. We can arrange to move the items to our place if you buy anything."

She purchased bamboo and wicker furniture, metal framed beds, floor mats and dressers for George Jr. and Barbara. She found a used metal desk for George Jr.'s quarters. Most of the kitchenware she also obtained at the moving sale.

As I wound my way along the base of Diamond Head toward downtown, the view swept through my soul, cracking the shell I had around my heart from my family's betrayal. Would it take eons for the hurt to erode? Maybe. Maybe decades. My anger still flared when I remembered.

Clouds brightened the sky and promised to keep the day cool. Wearing long sleeves to hide my tattoo often caused me to sweat excessively. Not today. Summer was not in a hurry.

I shifted into a higher gear in my retrofitted car, and then cleared my head to focus on the transition ahead. I'd had my car shipped from the mainland so I could drive to my new job. I had my work cut out. RCA handled most of the eastbound traffic because we had the strongest transmitter in the Pacific. Other companies on the island competed for the westbound and remaining eastbound traffic. Only three had wireless.

After introductions, the exiting manager explained, "Occasionally, the military use our services when they can't punch through the atmospheric disturbances that occurred at dawn. The Japanese Consulate also uses us because they can only receive wireless messages. They didn't have the equipment needed to transmit."

"Are the messages in code?" I asked.

"Usually. We insist that each word group contain a vowel, for easier keying. If it's not we charge more."

"How about Romaji? Romanized Japanese?"

"Yes. That too. Keeps the operators on their toes."

After Tom gave me a tour of our facilities, I requisitioned new equipment I'd become familiar with in New York. I also planned to reach out to my contacts in Japan and China to encourage an increase in traffic since the staff seemed very capable. My days became long but satisfying, and I looked forward to sharing the island breezes with my children during my time off. They had a lot of healing to do.

The children arrived on the 29th of August, bright-eyed and bushy-tailed, as Kay used to say. Kay offered to accompany them, but I didn't want her anywhere near them. A clean break is what they needed, not a weepy-eyed mother who blamed everyone but herself for her troubles. I gave Kay my office address so I could read her letters before I gave them to the children. I wouldn't allow her to impose her woefulness or misguided ways on them.

"*Aloha*, you are finally here," I said when I greeted them at the dock below the Aloha Tower. "We didn't say goodbye, so we are saying hello again."

"*Aloha*," they said in unison as Nina draped leis around their necks and gave each a peck on the cheek.

"Tell me all about your crossing." I'd arranged a berth for George Jr. with younger men headed to the island as contractors. Barbara was assigned to a room with three women. I paid extra so the purser would keep an eye on them.

"I was seasick," Barbara said, "but not for long. 'First call to breakfast' got me up every morning. My bunkmates tucked me in at night."

"Were they nice ladies?" I asked.

"Oh, yes, they waved to me when they saw me. I had a lot of fun with the other kids," she explained. "We played cards and ran around the ship. It was so much fun."

George Jr. said, "I kept an eye on her. We always ate our meals together."

"Well done, son," I said. "That's what men are supposed to do." He swelled with pride, and it dawned on me he hadn't had a man around to teach him how to be one. I would put an end to that. But how would I teach Barbara to be a woman? Kay's constant attempt to defy middle age and maturity certainly wasn't a good example for Barbara. Was Nina up to the task? She certainly hadn't had a lot of guidance from her family.

Hula dancers performed on the pier as we jostled luggage and made our way to customs. Barbara was captivated.

"Daddy, can I learn to hula dance?" she asked.

"*May* I learn to hula dance," I corrected. I might not be able to teach Barbara how to be a woman, but I could teach her proper English. "I don't see why not. You're in Hawaii now."

Nina interjected, "I mother now. We go to home. Discuss hula. You help maybe then get hula lessons."

I kept quiet. I wasn't sure what the children would think of Nina. They'd only seen her on a handful of occasions. A new mother? I hoped so. Their grandmothers had been the most stabilizing force in their lives, and my mother had betrayed their trust—and mine. I had talked to Nina about this during our crossing. We decided that the best thing to do was establish a routine, tell them the rules, and hold them accountable like adults.

"We family now," said Nina.

"She's right; we are a family now. Nina is your new mother, and you must do what she says. We will be home soon. You each have your own room, which we expect you to keep clean. There will be other chores. I have a job and will be gone most of the day. Nina will be in charge while I'm gone. That is her job. I expect you to do your jobs well, at school and at home."

Both were silent. Like puppies in a pet shop, they pressed their noses to the car windows as we wound around Diamond Head. When we pulled into the carport, Barbara frowned, visibly disappointed. "You said we had a little grass shack? It's like any other house."[122]

"I'll take you to see one, and you'll see why this is so much better," I said with a chuckle. "Let's get you unpacked, and Nina will walk you to the beach. It's a bit hard for me yet."

Over the next two weeks, before school started, Nina and I drove them around the island after they'd done their chores. They eagerly did as they were told and even expressed gratitude when we went exploring. When we were at home, there was no keeping them away from the beach. I could see the dreariness of the past diminish from their eyes with each receding wave as they romped in the surf. Slowly, they became more animated, bursting into the house to share their discoveries with me. Their skin bronzed. They reminded me of gazelles, all legs and high spirits. Homesickness didn't bother them. They'd had no home for years.

Left to right: Barbara, George, George Jr.1935 *(George Street Archive)*

"George Jr.," I said, remembering to not call him Georgie at his request, "How about building us a boat that I can ride in?"

"Well, how would I do that?" he asked. 'I've only made one wooden item, and it was small."

"I have tools. I'll show you how to use them. Go to the library and research designs."

He was off the next day, eager to please, and excited about building a boat. He returned with hand-drawn sketches he'd copied out of a book.

"What do you think, Dad?"

"Looks like it will work."

"Can I set up in the carport?"

"I don't know. Can you? The proper way to ask is, *"May* I set up in the carport?"

"May I set up in the carport?" George Jr. repeated.

"Sure," I said. "Give me a list of the wood you need, and I'll have the local lumber company deliver it. I'll double-check your numbers if you want."

He set sawhorses under the carport and cut each board by hand. I'd check his work, but he needed little instruction.

"Measure twice, cut once," I told him.

He was a natural. Barbara tried to help, but George Jr. wasn't willing to let her do too much. It was his project. In a matter of weeks, he'd completed a rowboat large enough for two. When the time came to launch it, Barbara christened it with a bottle of milk, carefully gathering the shards of glass off the beach. George Jr. eased his masterpiece into the surf, and we held our breaths.

"No leaks!" he exclaimed, and he hopped over the gunwale.

"Well done, son, well done," I said as Barbara pushed it further into the sea before scrambling aboard while George Jr. steadied the oars. He stayed close to the shore on their maiden voyage, just in case, but his grin said it all.

We sat around the table at dinner, chatting about the day's events. When Barbara spoke, Nina said, "You clear table. Girls be quiet; let men talk." Barbara rose and did as she was told without back talk, probably because I was there.

Nina demanded more and more of Barbara. She had her set the table, pass

George and Barbara in rowboat *(George Street Archive)*

the food, clear the table, do the dishes, and clean the kitchen. When I questioned Nina, she'd responded. "It what girls do. Barbara spoiled. She talk back. No go rowing until all chores done. It George Jr. boat."

I let it go. What did I know about raising girls? Barbara said she was happy. Her grades were good. She was taking hula lessons. What more was there?

George Jr., Barbara, and I rose to go to our sceened-in lanai He had grown and had developed some muscles in the last few month, no doubt from all the boating he did. I hired him as a back-up messenger boy when he wasn't at school. He filled-in several times a week now that traffic from Ft. Shafter and the Japanese Consulate had increased dramatically. He did a good job. Made me proud.

He plopped on one of the chairs reminding me of a sprawled cat basking in the sun.

"Daddy, what's this scar on your arm?" Barbara asked as she perched on the arm of my chair; apparently all her chores were done.

"Barbara, that's Nina spot." George Jr. interjected.

"I know. She's busy fixing desert. Besides, it's not her chair."

"You are tempting fate," I offered.

"I'll get up when she comes in. What is that scar on your arm?" she asked again.

Barbara had grown bolder and more self-confident since school started. I decided to let her impertinence go. If Nina objected she'd say something.

"That, Barbara, is one of my first big mistakes. It's a tattoo that became infected. I had to cut it out with a kitchen knife while at sea. There wasn't a doctor on board the ship. If I hadn't, blood poisoning would have killed me."

"Did it hurt to cut it out?"

"Oh, yes, it hurt. It was the worst hurt I'd ever felt. But I had to take care of it myself. No one else would. I made the mistake of getting the damn tattoo. It was up to me to fix it. Ma warned me about getting one. But I didn't listen."

"Grandma Street always used to say that I should pay attention to what she told me."

"Moms are right sometimes, but not always. What is important, no matter what, is to take responsibility for yourself, for what you do, and help those you love. Don't expect others to do things for you."

I wanted to say more. I wanted to let Barbara know that each created their own story, regardless of who they merge with. It would be up to her to navigate life's rough seas, to replace the missing link in her anchor chain when it snaps, and to cut out her own tattoo when it becomes septic. But she is still young. At least now, I could guide and protect her when the waves crashed upon her.

Or so I hoped.

I turned to George Jr. and said, "I need you to make the Ft. Shafter run tomorrow morning. The regular runner has a doctor's appointment. I'll drop you at school when we are done. I need you to be my legs."

"Okay. I like going on the Army base. Will the run include Pearl Harbor?"

"Yes, Shafter and Pearl Harbor. I'll be a few minutes at Shafter. I want to talk to the commanding officer about setting up a direct line from the Signal Corps office to RCA so we won't have to send a messenger. When we receive a radiogram for them they'd get it in seconds. It'd make things easier for both of us."

Nina joined us, glaring at Barbara for sitting in her spot.

Barbara rose and gave Nina a look.

A storm was brewing between the two. Like a typhoon gathering strength, they swirled around each other finding calm only when I intervened. At some point, they were bound to become a tempest of female hysteria. I prayed I wouldn't have to choose between the two.

"Remember—responsibility and respect," I said to Barbara. "Now, off you go. Go practice the hula, my little island girl."

Nina sat at my side. "What Barbara say?" she asked.

"Nothing. She wanted to know about my scar. Don't be so nosey."

Nina shifted to another chair, giving me a look. I picked up the newspaper to read about the Nazi Party forbidding Germans to marry Jews.

Such nonsense!

George Street 1935. Note the cane in the lower left-hand corner.

(George Street Archive)

Author's Note

The Street family story continues in *Pearl Harbor's Final Warning, A Man, a Message, and Paradise Lost.* Operational snafus, collusion, and spies weave a web of misdirection that entangles George and his children in one of history's biggest mistakes.

Pearl Harbors Final Warning was awarded the 2022 Gold Medal for History by the Military Writer's Society of America and the 2023 Silver Medal from the National Indie Excellence Award.

It is available through your local bookstore, library, Amazon, Barn's & Noble, Walmart, and Google Books.

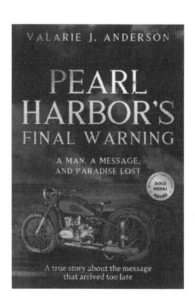

Praise for

Pearl Harbor's Final Warning

- *2022 Gold Medal winner for history from the Military Writer's Society of America*
- *2023 Silver Medal winner from the National Indie Excellence Awards*

- Splendid, top-notch, beautifully researched and documented...a real service to history and historians...*Scott S. UC Davis*

- ....best non-fiction book I've read...*Bob R. Archivist, Society of Wireless Pioneers and California Historical Radio Society*

- ...delighted to carry it...*Erickson Aviation Museum*

- I've read Gordon Prange's Dec. 7 book, but I learned more from yours. I was blown away by the level of detail! *Zach M. Editor- in- Chief of LST Scuttlebutt Magazine*

- This is a book that will hold you spell-bound... Each chapter leaves you clamoring to continue. *Nugget News*

- The book is meticulously researched...best nonfiction books I've read... reads like a spy thriller and gives a unique perspective on one aspect of the Second World War. *Linda W.*

- Your history is right on. *Old Salt (Horace Hamilton, Pearl Harbor Survivor)*

- This book should be read by every civic class student to obtain a better understanding of the sacrifices made for the good of the community and the nation. *Eric S.*

- "The Final Warning" is so interesting that I find it hard to put it down!" *Fred R. (Veteran)*

- A well written and well researched book...looks at the human side. What the citizens of Honolulu were doing and thinking before, during, and after the attack was very interesting to me. *Virginia S.*

There is nothing quite like the magic of a group of writers sitting around a table. Their faces read like an open book. Some reflect their most recent rejection. Others sparkle, bursting with news. All exude eagerness and the willingness to set aside ego and open themselves to the healing power of sharing and learning.

Our group, Sisters' Write, takes constructive criticism to heart, and we don't wrap their words with banal and misleading compliments. We understand that the easy part is writing, the tough part is editing. Without exception, Sisters' Write members opened their minds and ears and really listened, an art form that is rapidly disappearing into the world of tweets and texts.

It's this rare quality of honesty that shapes my writing and me. It was Sisters' Write that helped me weave the words that became *Sparks in the Ether*. They pushed and prodded me to create a work of creative non-fiction, guiding me through the quirks of dialog, reassuring me when I got it right, and bravely telling me when I missed the mark.

I always look forward to our weekly meetings, to the freshness of readable faces, to the strength they generate, and to the wisdom of their words. I can't thank them enough.

I'd also like thank my beta readers Bob Rydzewski, Scott Sibbett, Nancy Glaspie, Randy King, my brothers, James R. Olsen and Bill Olsen, my sister Kathy Klattenhoff and her husband Weldon. They improved this book greatly.

Men I have never met in person lent a helping hand. Scott Sibbett first reached out to me via my website. He introduced me to Bart Lee,

Mike Adams, Bob Rydzewski, and the California Historical Radio Society. We now meet once a month via Zoom to share research material relating to early radio. They all contributed greatly to my knowledge about wireless, and I thank them.

Later, Scott and I discovered his great-grandfather had formed a business with George Street in San Lorenzo, CA—*Sibbett & Street Sterilized Wiping Rags*. Scott was kind enough to provide a picture of their enterprise.

My deepest gratitude goes to George Street Jr. who spent countless hours sharing his stories and documentation before he died in 2022. He was one of the finest men I have ever known and will always remain in my heart.

My gratefulness also extends to my husband William, my children, and the Texas Twins and Comma Queens, Martha Collins and Nancy Glaspie, who encouraged and propelled me forward. I couldn't have written this without them. Unfortunately, Martha died before she could hold this book in her hands. I send my thanks to her in heaven. I was blessed to have known her and will miss her forever.

Bibliography

Backus, Bertha Adams. "Best-Loved Poems-American People." *www.amazon.com/Best Loved Poems.* c.1911. www.amazon.com/Best loved poems-American People/dp.038500197 (accessed September 13, 2013).

Balk, Alfred. *The Rise of Radio; From Marconi through the Golden Age.* Jefferson, North Carolina: McFarland & Company, Inc., 2006.

Brendon, Piers. *The Dark Valley, A panorama of the 1930s.* New York: Vintage ebook, 2007.

Brown, Robert J. *Manipulating the Ether;the Power of Broadcast Radio in the Thirties America.* Jefferson, North Carolina: McFarland & Company, Inc., 1998.

Carnes, Patrick J. *the Betrayal Bond; Breaking Free of Explitive Relationships.* Dearfield Beach, Florida: Health Communications, Inc., 1997.

Chen, Szu-Wei. *The Music Industry and Popular son in the 1930s and 1940s Shanghai, A historical and Stylistic Ananlysis.* PhD dissertation, Department of Film and Media Studies, University of Stirling, 2007.

Coe, Lewis. *Wireless Radio: A History.* Jefferson, NC: McFarland & Company, Inc. , 1996.

Foreign Relations of the United States 1931, The Far East, Vol. III. *(Washington Government Printing Office),* n.d.

Golden, Arthur. *Memoirs of a Geisha.* New York: Vintage Books, 1999.

Gose, Eileen Tannich and Kathy Wiederstein DeHerrera. *Reflecting Freedom: How Fashion Mirrored the Struggle for Women's Rights.* Charleston: Authors, 2017.

Horodysky, T. *American Merchant Marine at War: U.S. Merchant Ships Sunk or Damages in World War II.* January 21, 2004. (accessed April 2, 2020).

Johnson, Al. "The Pioneer Wireless Women, Stella J. Cayo." *Sparks Journal: Pioneer Wireless Society, Inc.*, 2012: 13.

Lyons, Eugene. *David Sarnoff; A Biography.* New York: Harper & Row, Publishers, 1966.

Newell, Gordon, and Joe Williamson. *Pacific Lumber Ships.* New York: Bonaza Books, 1960 by Superior Publishing Co.

Parker, Christian. *On a Single Stack Steamer;Plying Northwest Waters.* Chimacum, Washington: Olympic Dispatch, 2012.

Rydzewski, Robert. "The Wireless Boys of Alameda, Part 2-There Ought to Be a Law." *California Historical Radio Society Journal*, Spring/Summer 2022: 11 pages.

Seattle Times, Chicago Tribune, NY Times Special Services. "China-US Radio Draws Protest of Japan to Nanking." December 5, 1930.

Soennichsen, John. *Miwoks to Missiles, A History of Angel Island.* Tiburon, Ca.: Angel Island Association, 2005.

Street, George. " George Street Archives." unpublished, 1898-1995.

Street, Geroge Jr., and Valarie J. Anderson and Partrica March. *A Compendium of the Life and Times of George Street Sr.* Sisters, OR: unpublished, 2013.

Summerland Amateur Radio Club. "Radiotelegraph and Radiotelephone Codes, Prowords and Abbreviations (Third Edition)." 2002. (accessed May 15, 2020).

Todd, George P. "Early Radio Communications in the Fourteenth Naval District, Pearl Harbor, Territory of Hawaii." *Navy Radio.* 1985. (accessed February 2, 2020).

Trautman, Jim. *"The Lindberghs' Forgotten Flight to the Orient.".* September 2017. https://www.historynet.com/lindbergh-canada/#:~:text=In%201931%20the%20celebrated%20aviator,no%20records%20to%20be%20sought. (accessed January 30, 2023).

Tredree, H. L. *The Strange Ordeal of the Normandier.* Boston, MA: Little, Brown and Company, 1958.

Warner, J. C. *History of Radio Corporation of America.* One of a series of talks by RCA executives to members of their staffs., RCA, c.1937.

White, J. Andrew Editor. "Announcement." *Marconi Service News*, 1916: Vol 1, No 6.

Wright, E. W. *Lewis and Dryden's Marine History of the Pacific Northwest.* Forgotten Books: London, U.K., 2017.

Index

Endnotes

[1] Letter to Ma dated 4-16-1919, p. 5.

[2] George Street Archive, Diary.

[3] Street, Anderson, March, *Compendium*, p. 50, Letter to George Jr. dated 12-7-1974.

[4] As told to Kathy Klattenhoff.

[5] Street, Anderson, March, *Compendium*, p.22, Letter to George, Jr. dated 11-12-1969.

[6] Street, Anderson, March, *Compendium*, p.18, Letter to George, Jr. dated 4/11/1969.

[7] Letter to George Jr. dated 1973.

[8] Rydzewski, *The Wireless Boys of Alameda Part2-There Ought To Be a Law,* p. 27.

[9] Yerba Buena (Goat Island) Naval facility
https://www.history.navy.mil/content/history/nhhc/our-collections/photography/technology/communications/radio/ug-21--us-naval-california-radio-station-collection/yerba-buena--goat-island--naval-radio-station-.html
accessed 1-18-21

[10] Warner, *History of Radio Corporation of America.*

[11] Lyons, *David Sarnoff, A Biography.*

[12] Radio Museum, papers: *History of the Manufacturer Pacific Research Laboratorie,*https://www.radiomuseum.org/dsp_hersteller_detail.cfm?company_id=20964

[13] George Street Archive, Binder 3, 1944, p. 4, Speech.

[14] When the bridge later became a tunnel, Kay would hold her breath and take the author's hand.

[15] *Honolulu Star-Bulletin*, 16 August 1919, p. 13.

[16] *Ibid.*

[17] United States Department of the Interior, National Park Service, National Register of Historic Places Registration Form, p.14.

[18] Koko Head Report, RCA *World Wide Wireless* newsletter Vol.2, dated May 1921, p. 12.

[19] *Honolulu Advertiser*, 11 July 1920, p. 25.

[20] Koko Head, Oahu report, RCA *World Wide Wireless* newsletter Vol. 2, dated January 2021, p. 25.

[21] *Honolulu Advertiser*, 8 November 1921, p.10.

[22] Koko Head, Oahu report, RCA *World Wide Wireless* newsletter Vol. 2, dated May 1921, p. 12.

[23] Street, Anderson, March, *Compendium*, pg. 63.

[24] The tea cup is now with the author.

[25] Street, Anderson, March, *Compendium*, pgs. 52-53 Capwell, *Sea Goin' Wireless* clipped article from H.C. Capwell publication Progress, 1921.

[26] George Street Archive, diary.

[27] Rydzewski, *The Wireless Boys of Alameda Part 2-There Ought To Be a Law,* p.20.

[28] Ibid.

[29] Street, Anderson, March, *Compendium*, pg.33.

[30] Ibid, p.32.

[31] Ibid.

[32] Ibid, p.33.

[33] *San Francisco Call*, Vol. 99, Num. 24, 24 December 1905.
[34] Melendy, *Vivilore,* p. 275-6.
[35] Koko Head report, RCA *World Wide Wireless* newsletter Vol. 2, dated September 1921, p.26.
[36] Kahuku, Oahu, T. H. report, RCA *World Wide Wireless* newsletter Vol. 3, dated March 1922, p. 20.
[37] Kahuku report, RCA *World Wide Wireless* newsletter Vol. 3, dated July 1922, p. 13.
[38] Honolulu City office report, RCA *World Wide Wireless* newsletter Vol 3, dated March 1922, p. 23.
[39] *Seattle Star*, 7 August 1925.
[40] Street, Anderson, March, *Compendium*, p. 71. Letter to Barbara Jean dated 11-16-73.
[41] Now called faxes.
[42] Street, Anderson, March, *Compendium*, p. 77. Letter to George Jr. dated 11-18-66.
[43] George Street Archive, Binder 1, 1926, p. 2; Letter dated 18 Nov 1966.
[44] *The Morning Oregonian*, 16 August 1926.
[45] Balk, *The Rise of Radio*, p. 68.
[46] Street, Anderson, March, *Compendium*, p. 68, interview with George Jr.
[47] Johnson, The Pioneer Wireless Women; Stella J. Cayo, *Sparks Journal*, p.13.
[48] George Street Archive, Binder 1, 1927, p. 4; Letter dated 23 August 1927.
[49] George Street Archive, Binder 2, 1930, p. 5; Memo from General Superintendent, T. M. Stevens dated 11 November 1930.
[50] Antitrust issues in the United States prevented the sale.
[51] Interview with George Street Jr.
[52] George Street Archive, Binder 2, p. 5a, 1930 letter to A.A. Isbell.
[53] Backus, *Then Laugh* c 1911 courtesy Patricia March.
[54] George Street Archive, Binder 2, 1931, Letter from Shecklen dated 12 April 1931.
[55] Street, Anderson, March, *Compendium*, p. 95.
[56] Chen, "The Music Industry and Popular Song in the 1930s and 1940s Shanghai, A Historical and Stylistic Analysis."
[57] Brendon, *The Dark Valley; A Panorama of the 1930s*; Bickers, *Empire Made Me: An Englishman Adrift in Shanghai,* p.59.
[58] *North-China Daily News*, Vol. CXXII No. 20163, 2 Feb 1930. Percival Phillips was a famous American journalist and war correspondent knighted by the Queen of England.
[59] *Shanghai Sunday Times*, "Hoover and Chiang Kai-shek Exchange Messages," (clipping George Street Archive)
[60] Also known as Peking, now Beijing.
[61] George Street Achieve, Binder 2, 1931, p. 14; Report to E. J Nally dated 17 June 1931.
[62] George Street Archive, clipping; *Seattle Times-Chicago Tribune*- N.Y. Times Special Service December 5 (no year on clipping), probably 1931.
[63] George Street Achieve, Binder 2, 1931, p. 14; Report to E. J Nally dated 17 June 1931.
[64] George Street Archive, Binder 2, p. 9 Memo from R.R. Beal dated 4-30-1931.
[65] *China News*," George Street Honorary Advisor to the Minister of Communications, National Government of China.," 3 July 1931.
[66] George Street Archive, Binder 2, p.14 Report to E. J. Nally dated June 17, 1931 (p.4).
[67] George Street Archive, Photo album.
[68] George Street Archive, Binder 2, 1931, p 6; "Shanghai Overcast-A Busy Saturday Morning," by George Street.
[69] George Street Archive, Binder 2, 1931, p. 1; Letter from Shecklen dated 12 April 1931.
[70] Truman, "The Lindbergh's' Forgotten Flight to the Orient."

[71] George Street Archive, Binder 2, 1931, p. 6, "Shanghai Overcast, A Busy Saturday Morning" by George Street.

[72] George Street Archive, Binder 2, 1931, p 6; "Shanghai Overcast-A Busy Saturday Morning," by George Street.

[73] George Street Archive, Binder 2, 1931, p. 23, Letter to Ma dated 16 October 1931.

[74] George Street Archive, Binder 2, 1931, p. 14; Report to E. J Nally dated 17 June 1931.

[75] George Street Archive, Binder 2, 1932, p. 29.

[76] Street, Anderson, March, *Compendium*, p. 109.

[77] George Street Archive, Binder 2, 1932, p. 9, *RCA News*, Vol. 13, April 1932.

[78] Street, Anderson, March, *Compendium*, p. 105, Letter to Barbara dated 9-13-1972.

[79] Ibid.

[80] Ibid.

[81] Street, Anderson, March, *Compendium*, p. 107 Letter to Barbara dated 9-13-72.

[82] Foreign Relations of the United States, The Far East, Vol. III, Memorandum by Consul General Shanghai 25 January 1932.

[83] *Oakland Tribune* "Shanghai In Terror; 29 Die in Blast," Oakland, Ca. 25 January 1932.

[84] Ibid, 27, January memorandum.

[85] George Street Achieve, Binder 2, 1932, p.10b; Letter to Ma dated 12 March 1932.

[86] Foreign Relations of the United States, The Far East, Vol. III, Memorandum to Consul General Shanghai, 2-11 March 1932.

[87] Letter to Barbara (Street) Olsen, dated January13,1973; source: Kathy Kattenhoff

[88] Street, Anderson, March, *Compendium*, p. 113, Letter to Mr. Winterbottom dated 7-9-1932.

[89] Ibid.

[90] Ibid.

[91] Ibid.

[92] George Street Archive, Binder 2, 1932, p. 11.

[93] George Street Archive, Binder 2, 1931, p.12.

[94] Ibid, p.11.

[95] Ibid, p.13.

[96] Ibid, p.14.

[97] There was no health insurance, disability insurance, workman's compensation, or unemployment insurance in 1932.

[98] George Street Archive, Binder 2, 1932, p.17.

[99] Ibid, p.21

[100] Ibid.

[101] Refrain by Arthur V. Olsen overheard by the author.

[102] George Street Archive, Binder 2, 1932, p. 21.

[103] Ibid, p.7.

[104] Ibid, p 21.

[105] Most likely, the Sister Kenny treatment method developed in Australia.

[106] Nina Street Binder, 1932, Letter to American Consul General from Mrs. A. E. Zaeff, dated 23 August 1932.

[107] George Street Archive, Binder 2, 1932, p. 21.

[108] Ibid, p. 25.

[109] Ibid, p. 26.

[110] Ibid.

[111] Ibid.

[112] Ibid.

[113] Ibid, p. 27.
[114] Street, Anderson, March, *Compendium*, p. 62.
[115] George Street Archive, Binder 2, 1933, p.5.
[116] George Street Archive, Binder 2, 1934, p. 1.
[117] George Street Archive, Binder 2, p. 3.
[118] Hawaiian slang for Coca-Cola.
[119] Street, Anderson, March, *Compendium*, pgs. 128-129, undated letter to Barbara.
[120] George Street Archive Binder 2, 1935, p. 4.
[121] Interview with George Jr., 2021.
[122] Interview with Barbara, 2011.

Made in United States
Troutdale, OR
02/06/2024

17345203R10159